AND THE WORD

Became Flesh

A 90-DAY CHRONOLOGICAL JOURNEY THROUGH THE NEW TESTAMENT

by Kathy L. Gossen

And the Word Became Flesh:
A 90-Day Chronological Journey Through the New
Testament

First printing 2014
Printed in the United States of America
ISBN-13: 978-1497466258

ISBN-10: 1497466253

Dewey Decimal Number: 232
Subject Heading: CHRISTIAN LIVING/SPIRITUAL GROWTH

To my parents, Ray and Karen Cripps, the first people to show me God's love in action, pray for me, and believe in me. I love you both.

Contents

Introduction

"And the word became flesh, and dwelt among us" (John 1:14). I don't think I ever fully grasped the meaning behind that verse until I completed this New Testament journey. There were so many times the scriptures came alive to me throughout this study such that I was immediately convicted to do or act differently in my daily life. Yet that's exactly what the scripture is supposed to do – change us. "And the word became flesh…" – the Word is to be lived out in human flesh so others can see it – first in Jesus and now in us. My hope is that this study changes you spiritually, mentally, and emotionally so that you become more like Christ and others can see the change in you.

For this study I highly encourage using a journal to write down your responses to the reflection questions and/or record your prayers. Taking the time to write down your prayers can help you focus on what you are praying and also reveal how God is truly at work in your life when prayers are answered. Recording responses to the reflection questions can also bring into the spotlight certain concerns or challenges you may otherwise skip over. Personally, I also enjoy reviewing my responses during the next time I complete the same study to see how my time with Jesus has caused me to grow and change.

I also recommend index cards to record and review your weekly memory verses. Place these cards in a prominent place such as near your kitchen or bathroom sink or the dash of your car where you can quickly review them while simultaneously completing another task. If you have already memorized the verse of the week, feel free to choose another key verse from the week or another favorite verse from the passages you are reading. The choice is up to you. The goal is to just continually hide His Word in your heart so that He will be able to help you recall them when you need them most (Psalm 119:11).

I enjoyed creating this study as it allows you to work on a variety of Christian disciplines (Bible study, reflection, prayer, and scripture memory) in one swoop while providing enough flexibility that a reader can choose to include or not include specific aspects of the study as desired. My hope is that this journey will allow you to not only read through the New Testament in 90 days, but be transformed by the Word as you take time for reflection, prayer, and scripture memory based on what you are reading. May the Bible come alive within you like never before. May the Word become flesh in you so that others may see His love and glorify the Father in heaven for sending His Son to save them.

Week 1

And Jesus kept increasing in wisdom and stature, and in favor with God and men. Luke 2:52

Day 1

And the Word became flesh, and dwelt among us, and we saw His glory, glory as of the only begotten from the Father, full of grace and truth. John 1:14

Day's Reading: Luke 1, John 1:1-14

The gospel of Luke is the favorite gospel of many, especially when it comes to the story of the birth of Christ, because of the extreme detail Luke provides to every scenario. Yet, unlike the other gospel writers, he never met Jesus during his earthly ministry. Instead he gathered his information from other eye witnesses and personal testimonies. In addition, Luke is also considered the only Gentile author of the New Testament, making his angle of grace that much more potent.   Thanks to his love for detail, the gospel of Luke is the longest of the gospels and the only gospel with a sequel — Acts. Luke wrote this gospel to a man named Theolophilus during the time of Nero, when Christians were being terribly persecuted. While the other gospels were written for area churches, Luke's primary intent was to give Theolophilus, who was most likely a new Gentile convert, examples of Christ's power and God's grace as a means to reassure him of his beliefs during a time of great trial.

Reflection:

- How would you have responded to Gabriel's visit if you had been Mary or Zacharias?
- How would you have responded to Mary's or Zacharias' testimony if you had been a close friend listening first hand to their story?
- Have you ever had a situation like Mary and Zacharias where you came in contact with the Lord in

such a personal way that you couldn't help but sing a song about it or proclaim God's good news?

Prayer Guide:

- Thank Him for the coming of the Christ-child and His miraculous revelations.
- Ask for greater love for the Lord much like Mary and Zacharias had as a result of coming in contact with God's messenger.
- Express your desire for personal spiritual growth, sensitivity to sin, and discipline to maintain a daily quiet time.
- Intercede for your spouse's spiritual growth, sensitivity to sin, and spiritual leadership.
- Pray for your children's spiritual growth and sensitivity to sin.
- Submit your day's activities to Him.

Memory Verse Goals:

- Read the verse of the week five times.
- Post the verse of the week in a prominent location.

Day 2

"Behold, the virgin shall be with child and shall bear a Son, and they shall call His name Immanuel," which translated means, "God with us." Matthew 1:23

Day's Reading: Matthew 1, Luke 2:1-38

Several years ago the movie *Catch Me If You Can* told the story of Frank Abagnale and how he was able to con millions as a pilot, doctor, and lawyer. When finally caught, he was asked how to tell counterfeit money from the real deal. He replied something like "Simple. You study the real McCoy." Mathew is much like the real McCoy. He wants to make sure his readers know that Jesus is the real deal and not just another imposter.

Although the book never mentions the author directly, it is assumed that the disciple Matthew wrote the book based on its distinctly Jewish overtones, strong emphasis on money (he was a tax collector), and frequent descriptions given when mentioning Capernaum, his hometown.

From the detailed genealogy at the beginning to the Great Commission at the end, this disciple uses his background, personal experiences and God-given purpose to prove Jesus is who He said He was by highlighting his teaching and righteous life, outlining true characteristics of the kingdom of God (some thought he was not the Messiah because his kingdom didn't come to fruition on earth), and instructing the church via narratives of Jesus to further the gospel. Through Matthew's account we are assured Jesus really is the King of Kings and Lord of Lords. Hallelujah!

Reflection:

- What names stood out to you as you read the genealogy of Christ? Why?
- Consider taking one meal time today to fast and pray as Anna did in the temple, giving thanks for the salvation of Jesus and praying for ways to further share the Good News with others.

Prayer Guide:

- Thank God for sending His Son and for using sinful women like Rahab to bring to fruition God's promise of redemption.
- Request wisdom for you, your spouse, and your children regarding your time, talents, spiritual gifts, and finances.
- Pray for your immediate family members' and relatives' prayer requests/needs.
- Submit your day's activities to Him.

Memory Verse Goals:

- Look up any unfamiliar words or meanings found in the verse of the week.
- Pray and meditate on the verse of the week.

Day 3

The Child continued to grow and become strong, increasing in wisdom; and the grace of God was upon Him. Luke 2:40

Day's Reading: Matthew 2, Luke 2:39-52

When envisioning the story of the wise men, many put them in the same picture as the shepherds alongside the manger scene much like the picture perfect nativity scenes seen on many a mantle around Christmastime. However, as Matthew points out Jesus was a young Child (vs. 8) at this time living in a house (v. 11) not the often misconceived baby in a stable from chapter 1.

It is amazing to watch the story unfold as the gifts of the wise men most likely provided the financial resources needed for Joseph, Mary, and Jesus to travel to Egypt and finally Nazareth (their hometown where the story began in chapter 1), while guided by four dreams from heaven (vs. 12, 13, 19, 22). Oh, what amazing stories Joseph must have been able to tell his children as they grew.

Reflection:

- Imagine you were Joseph during this time. How would you feel having been divinely intercepted four times by a dream?
- How do you think the community of Nazareth responded when Joseph and his family returned to the place where the rumors of his "illegitimate" son all began?
- Ponder how you can instill a greater love and knowledge of God's Word in your children today.

Prayer Guide:

- Intercede for your children that they would grow "in wisdom and stature and in favor with God and man" just as Jesus did.
- Ask for an understanding of God's Word that leads to personal application.
- Pray for your friends' prayer requests/needs.
- Request wisdom regarding your children's friendships and influences.
- Submit your day's activities to Him.

Memory Verse Goals:

- Repeat the verse of the week phrase by phrase five times.

Day 4

"The time is fulfilled, and the kingdom of God is at hand; repent and believe in the gospel." Mark 1:15

Day's Reading: Matthew 3, Mark 1, Luke 3

The gospel of Mark could be summed up as "God is amazing! There is no other like Him!" It's the meaning of "gospel" to the core—"the Good News!"

Probably penned during the time of Nero's persecution and most likely after Paul's and Peter's death, Mark writes this gospel to encourage Roman believers during Nero's persecutions. As such, he neither assumes knowledge of the Old Testament or Jewish customs, explaining all as he writes making this passage an easier read for those just being introduced to the Good News.

Often credited as Peter's memoir with a few of Mark's personal stories sprinkled in, this gospel almost has the feel of an action-packed novel with its frequent use of "immediately" and quick transitions to the next event. As such, Mark focuses on Jesus' miracles as the Savior-King from the eyes of an on-the-scene reporter rather than someone just recording facts and teachings of Jesus. Mark's purpose—to transform lives, not just inform his readers.

Reflection:

- How does the disciples' response to Jesus motivate you in your relationship with Him today? Is there an area in your life in which you need to respond to Him immediately as opposed to when it is convenient?
- How would you respond to Jesus if you had been Simon or one of the other disciples? Would you have immediately dropped what you were doing and

followed Jesus or would you have had to wait until it was "just the right time"?

Prayer Guide:

- Ask for motivation to respond immediately to God's calling.
- Share with Him your heart—that you desire it to be filled with greater love and compassion for your children, your spouse, and those around you.
- Surrender your spouse's heart--that it would be filled with greater love and compassion for you and your children.
- Relinquish your children's hearts—that they would be filled with greater love and compassion for their siblings and others.
- Submit your day's activities to Him.

Memory Verse Goals:

- Say the verse of the week aloud twenty times in a row.

Day 5

The next day he saw Jesus coming to him and said, "Behold, the Lamb of God who takes away the sin of the world!" John 1:29

Day's Reading: Matthew 4, Luke 4-5, John 1:15-51

Growing up I was often encouraged to read the Gospel of John before reading through the rest of the Bible and with good reason. The Book of John is the only book written specifically as a guide to eternal life. John 3:16, probably the most famous of all Bible verses, is a prime example of this. As John states, we can have eternal life if we believe Jesus is the Son of God and Savior of the world.

The book of John was most likely written near the end of John's life. After the death of all the other disciples, John probably felt the increased importance to get the Word out as much as possible before his own death. His message is urgent and purposeful. He constantly points to Jesus' deity through "I am" statements, miraculous signs and other individuals' testimonies. Yes, truly Jesus is the Son of God so repent and believe!

Reflection:

- Have you chosen to believe in Jesus as your Savior? If so, thank God for His amazing gift. If not, I encourage you to make this life-changing decision today because as John says, He truly is "the Lamb of God who takes away the sin of the world" (John 1:29). That includes the sin of you and me; oh how freeing to know our salvation is not by works so that no one can boast (Ephesians 2:9), but by faith in Jesus Christ, the Son of God alone.

Prayer Guide:

- Thank God for sending His Son as the Savior of the world — of you.
- Pray for your and your spouse's safety, purity, and power to resist sexual and/or emotional temptation.
- Request help regarding your children's safety, wisdom, and purity.
- Pray for the safety and wisdom for the military and those you know in the military.
- Submit your day's activities to Him.

Memory Verse Goals:

- Review the verse of the week ten times in a row.

Day 6

Jesus answered and said to him, "Truly, truly, I say to you,
unless one is born again he cannot see the kingdom of God."
John 3:3

Day's Reading: John 2-4

Nicodemus was a Pharisee. Pharisees were the men who
were supposedly the "most qualified" to recognize the long-
awaited Messiah. Yet for many, their devotion to scripture
became their own concocted idol so much so that they exalted
themselves as a result of their "faith" and "truth." It kind of
reminds me of those who play the role of a "Christian" at
church because it will gain them social contacts or business
marketing opportunities rather than a deepening relationship
with Christ and His followers.

Nicodemus was found teetering between these two
worlds. How hard it must have been to give up his religious
rituals and hopes of the Messiah raising him up when
confronted with the truth found in Jesus. Yet Jesus loved him
through it all, and in the end Nicodemus was one of the first
on the scene to lovingly care for Jesus' body upon His death
(John 19:39-42). Yes, it took awhile for Nicodemus to take a
stand as one who had come into the light (John 3:21), but in
the end, he made the public choice which turned out to be the
right choice.

Reflection:

- Do you ever behave like the Pharisees, being
  religiously correct but forgetting the heart of Jesus?
  Has your religion ever become more of a social or
  selfish act rather than a humbling spiritual one?

- Do you ever find it hard to take a stand for Jesus in front of others in a way that brings Him glory, not you?
- Are you willing to expose your sins to others as the Samaritan woman did to her people so that Jesus may be proclaimed?

Prayer Guide:

- Request boldness to share Jesus with others despite your own short-comings.
- Ask for opportunities and confidence to show your spouse respect, grace, and kindness every day.
- Intercede for your children — that they would develop a heart of compassion, service, and prayer.
- Plead with God on behalf of the poor, hungry, and persecuted.
- Dedicate to God personally known city, state, national, and international mission efforts.
- Submit your day's activities to Him.

Memory Verse Goals:

- Review the verse of the week three times in a row.

Day 7

And hearing this, Jesus said to them, "It is not those who are healthy who need a physician, but those who are sick; I did not come to call the righteous, but sinners." Mark 2:17

Day's Reading: Mark 2

"When He had come back to Capernaum several days afterward, it was heard that He was at home." (Mark 2:1). While some assume Jesus was a homeless wanderer, time and again Capernaum is mentioned as Jesus' hub or where Jesus (along with his family and disciples) established his home during his ministry years. Need some proof? Take a look at Matthew 4:13 and John 2:12. Yes, although He traveled a lot, Jesus did have a hometown. What's even more interesting is to review all the miracles and events that took place in Capernaum. Capernaum was where the Centurion's servant was healed (Matthew 8:5-13), where he cast out an unclean spirit (Mark 1:21-28), where he healed the paralytic who was lowered through a roof (Mark 2:1-12), where he healed the nobleman's son who was miraculously healed from a distance (John 4:47-51) where Jesus walked on water (John 6:16-19), and more. Yes, a lot happened in Capernaum.

Yet, Capernaum was a sinful place (Matthew 11:23-24) — disgusting in God's eye. Maybe that's one reason why Jesus settled there because "it is not those who are healthy who need a physician, but those who are sick" (Mark 2:17). He had mercy even for a town doomed to destruction. Today, Capernaum is little more than a memorial to Jesus; the town is now completely gone just as Jesus promised.

Reflection:

- How do you think you would have responded to Jesus if you had lived in Capernaum the same time Jesus lived there?
- Why do you think Capernaum ultimately rejected Jesus despite his dwelling there? Do you think there is a connection between why Capernaum rejected Jesus and why so many others reject Jesus today? If so, what?

Prayer Guide:

- Thank God for His mercy for you, the sinner, and for coming to save you and draw you to repentance much as He did the town of Capernaum.
- Praise God for personal spiritual victories found in your life and those around you.
- Relinquish to God each immediate family member's self-confidence and self-motivation to do and be what He wants them to be.
- Pray for your church and the leadership therein.
- Submit your day's activities to Him.

Memory Verse Goals:

- Review the verse of the week one time.

Week 2

Let your light shine before men in such a way that they may see your good works, and glorify your Father who is in heaven. Matthew 5:16

Day 8

"Truly, truly, I say to you, he who hears My word, and believes Him who sent Me, has eternal life, and does not come into judgment, but has passed out of death into life."
John 5:24

Day's Reading: John 5

Christianity--what a misunderstood religion. Many believe America is a Christian nation (which it's not) and that Americans are Christians because they are Americans (which they are not) or that they are Christians because they go to church occasionally (which could not be further from the truth). Yes, many "Christians" are fakes making this whole "Christianity" thing somewhat confusing in our current culture to Christians and non-Christians alike.

Even Jesus came face to face with this problem during his ministry. Many Jews had come to accept their Jewish-ness as a cultural group rather than a belief. As Jesus said, "For if you believed in Moses you would believe in Me..." (John 5:46). In other words, you say you believe with your mouth, but the truth is not in you (Romans 10:9). Oh how deceived many will feel when they get to heaven if someone doesn't tell them the truth and set the record straight. Christianity isn't about the emblems or the attire or the denomination or the association. It's about a belief in a Savior who is Christ the Lord—a Savior that changes lives.

Reflection:

- What about you? Is your faith real? How do you know?
- How can we as "truth believing" Christians combat the fakeness of Christianity that has become so

prevalent in our society in an effort to draw others to Jesus, not away from Him?

Prayer Guide:

- Express your desire for a sincerity of faith.
- Share with Him your longing for a heart filled with worship.
- Request His leadership regarding your family, your family's activities, and your family's goals.
- Ask for discipline to accomplish your personal goals, Lord willing.
- Submit your day's activities to Him.

Memory Verse Goals:

- Read the verse of the week five times.
- Post the verse of the week in a prominent location.

Day 9

And He was saying to them, "The Son of Man is Lord of the Sabbath." Luke 6:5

Day's Reading: Matthew 12:1-21, Mark 3, Luke 6

One of the big hang-ups of the Pharisees was the observation of the Sabbath. They even created 39 categories of laws around the Sabbath. If they broke one of these laws, judgment would surely fall. While a few states and countries still have Blue Laws today (such as no selling of cars or liquor on Sundays), for the most part Christians today are free to enjoy the Sabbath however they please which can be both good and bad. In fact, some have chosen to not observe any form of Sabbath rest because they consider it an "Old Testament thing."

However, nothing could be further from the truth. Jesus didn't come to take away the Sabbath but to put it back into perspective for "the Sabbath was made for man not the man for the Sabbath" (Mark 2:28). We need the opportunity to rest and do good. As a matter of fact, in the busy 21st century, a Sabbath is not only encouraged but necessary for life, for health, and for freedom. How you choose to observe the Sabbath is up to you, but remember, the Sabbath day is a holy day designed by God at the dawn of creation. Use it to glorify Him in all you do.

Reflection:

- When do you take a Sabbath rest? How have you and/or will you choose to separate the day to do good, both for yourself and others?
- "I desire mercy and not sacrifice...." (Matthew 12:7). What do you think this means in light of the verses read today?

Prayer Guide:

- Thank God for a God-given time to rest and ask how you can use it to best glorify Him.
- Pray for a development of an eternal perspective in you and your family members.
- Request health and salvation for your family members.
- Ask for wisdom in teaching your children about loyalty and responsibility.
- Submit your day's activities to Him.

Memory Verse Goals:

- Look up any unfamiliar words or meanings found in the verse of the week.
- Pray and meditate on the verse of the week.

Day 10

"But seek first His kingdom and His righteousness, and all these things will be added to you." Matthew 6:33

Day's Reading: Matthew 5-7

Commonly known as the Sermon on the Mount, Matthew 5-7 provides solid instruction for Christian living. Intended for the ears of his disciples, this "sermon" was probably told to them many times so as to engrain it on their hearts. As such, of all the passages in the Bible, this is one we'd do well to read many times, if not memorize, so as to remind us as followers of Jesus what really matters.

Reflection:

- What guide for living found in these verses did God use to speak to you today? How will you strive to live changed after reading it?
- Consider reading this passage daily for a month each year or memorizing this passage over a period of a few months so as to engrain Jesus' heart within your own.

Prayer Guide:

- Begin today's prayer by reciting "The Lord's Prayer" (Matthew 6:9-13).
- Ask for an understanding of God's Word that leads to personal application.
- Request spiritual, mental, and emotional health for you and your family members.
- Pray for your neighbors' prayer requests/needs.
- Submit your day's activities to Him.

Memory Verse Goals:

- Repeat the verse of the week phrase by phrase five times.

Day 11

And He said to the woman, "Your faith has saved you; go in peace." Luke 7:50

Day's Reading: Matthew 8:1-13, Luke 7

The reading of today's passage reminds me of a few friends whom I've tried to talk to about Jesus. Their response? "I'm too sinful that anyone, even Jesus, could love and forgive me. You have no idea all the things I've done." To them I say time and again, "Oh but how much greater is His grace than your sin!" Maybe the next time such a conversation comes up I should pull out this passage of the sinful woman who was forgiven much. Can you imagine having the complete brokenness, humility of heart, and courage that this woman possessed to perform the deed she did in front of a Pharisee, let alone a crowd?

Reflection:

- Have you ever been in a place in your life in which you felt completely humble before the Lord asking forgiveness? If so, how has your life changed since?
- Whom do you know who might be interested in hearing the story of complete humility of the sinful woman? Make plans today to visit that person and share what God has been teaching you.

Prayer Guide:

- Thank God for His grace and love.
- Ask for faith like the centurion.
- Request wisdom regarding your family's finances and discipline to use the money God's given you for His glory.

- Pray for the moral integrity of the next generation.
- Surrender to God your children's future mates.
- Submit your day's activities to Him.

Memory Verse Goals:

- Say the verse of the week aloud twenty times in a row.

Day 12

"Come to Me, all who are weary and heavy-laden, and I will give you rest." Matthew 11:28

Day's Reading: Matthew 11

In this fast-paced life we've come to call the 21st century, life is stressful! People are constantly on the go and pressures constantly mount. In fact, I've heard it said that nearly a third of all Americans today have high blood pressure and nearly two-thirds of those require some form of medicine to control it. Conclusion: Sometimes life is a burden.

The Jews of Jesus' time were under a lot of pressure too, but of a different kind—the pressure of what the Pharisees and other religious leaders generally coded as "the law." They were tired and worn out from trying to keep up with it all, and unbeknownst to them, it wasn't even all God's design. Today we have pressure to do this or be that for society's approval, but how much more stressful might it have been if you felt you had to do something or be something for God's approval (whether true or not)? Oh, how blessed we are to know a gracious God who sent His Son to set the record straight.

Reflection:

- What can you let go today to lighten your load?
- Do you carry any religious "laws" around with you that many consider politically correct as a staunch Christian of society, but may not be biblically sound or loving in nature as God originally designed? If so, pray and give them to Jesus.

Prayer Guide:

- Thank God for the gracious gift of His Son who came to give us rest for our souls.
- Give any burdens to God that you are still unnecessarily carrying.
- Request physical strength and health for you, your spouse, and your children.
- Surrender to God your city, state, and national governments and the current issues therein.
- Pray for world leaders, events, and concerns.
- Submit your day's activities to Him.

Memory Verse Goals:

- Review the verse of the week ten times in a row.
- Review Luke 2:52 (from week 1) two times.

Day 13

Woe to you lawyers! For you have taken away the key of knowledge; you yourselves did not enter, and you hindered those who were entering." Luke 11:52

Day's Reading: Matthew 12:22-50, Luke 11

You may be looking at today's verse and thinking, "of all the verses in this passage why did Kathy choose to focus on that one?" Well, let's rephrase it a bit, shall we?

Woe to you "Christians"! For you have taken away the knowledge of Jesus from those who might have known. Now, because of your behavior and stubborn traditions, you will not enter heaven and neither will those with whom you could have shared the Good News.

Ouch! I don't know about you but that definitely hits a little closer to home for me. Oh how I pray that my life will not be so caught up in the "action" of being a Christian but in the faith, love and sincerity that comes from being a devout follower of Jesus. Even more, may I not hinder someone else from coming to known Him. Instead, may I be a sincere Christian in word and deed (James 1:22) not as a result of fashion or convenience but out of love for Him who saved me.

Reflection:

- Do you currently have any stumbling blocks in your life that you need to give over to God both for your sake and for the impact it can have on others for eternity? If so, pray that God will take them away and then develop a step-by-step plan to gradually remove those stumbling blocks from your path, if they are something which you are going to have to work at alongside God. Remember, some things you may be able to remove right away; others may take weeks, months, or even years to remove. Either way, keep at it because as Luke 11:8 declares, persistence will win out in the end.

Prayer Guide:

- Express your desire for a sincerity of faith.
- Request forgiveness for ever "putting on the show" or "faking it" as a Christian for the opinions of others.
- Ask for the Lord's blessing/enablement in your family's life roles.
- Pray for your family's energy, enthusiasm, and success in career settings.
- Surrender to God your children's education and those involved in their education.
- Submit your day's activities to Him.

Memory Verse Goals:

- Review the verse of the week three times in a row.
- Review Luke 2:52 (from week 1) one time.

Day 14

"But blessed are your eyes, because they see; and your ears, because they hear." Matthew 13:16

Day's Reading: Matthew 13, Luke 8

Jesus used parables much like other rabbis of the time to teach new truths about the kingdom using common every day scenes. In all, Jesus shares over 30 parables throughout the gospels to get his message across.

Today's parables are all about the value of heaven and how the wise will do anything to obtain it. How badly do you want to go to heaven? Are you willing to give everything you have away if that is what Jesus asked? If so, see Matthew 19:21.

Reflection:

- Which parable spoke most to you today? Why?
- How would you have responded to Jesus if you had been Mary or one of Jesus' brothers who had come to visit? (Luke 8:19-21)

Prayer Guide:

- Express your desire to be good soil that spreads the Good News.
- Request understanding regarding the mysteries of the kingdom.
- Ask for boldness and sensitivity to reach the lost and needy around you.
- Dedicate your church's ministries to Him.
- Pray for sensitivity to serve where needed in your community and/or church.

- Submit your day's activities to Him.

Memory Verse Goals:

- Review the verse of the week one time.
- Review Luke 2:52 (from week 1) one time.

Week 3

And He summoned the crowd with His disciples, and said to them, "If anyone wishes to come after Me, he must deny himself, and take up his cross and follow Me." Mark 8:34

Day 15

And He did not let him, but He said to him, "Go home to your people and report to them what great things the Lord has done for you, and how He had mercy on you." Mark 5:19

Day's Reading: Matthew 8:14-34, Mark 4-5

More than any other gospel, Mark uses examples of Jesus' miracles to tell about his amazing Savior. To be exact, he uses eighteen miracles to demonstrate Jesus' power over death, disease, evil forces, and even nature so that his readers are left knowing that there is no doubt that this Jesus must be the Messiah.

Mark also mentions three disciples whom Jesus probably considered his best friends — Peter, James, and John (Mark 5:37). It is these same disciples who also saw the Transfiguration (Mark 9:2) and accompanied Jesus for prayer in Gethsemane (Mark 14:32, 33). Yes, even Jesus, though God-Messiah, needed friends and longed for close companionship. But then, He still longs for it with us even today. Can you imagine? You, as a follower of Jesus Christ, have the opportunity to be close friends with the most miraculous man who ever lived. You can be friends with Jesus!

Reflection:

- How would you have responded if you had been one to witness some of Jesus' miracles?
- Do you take time each day to develop your friendship with Jesus? Hopefully yes, if you are doing this study. However, remember, as with any friendship, communication involves a two-way street. Take time today to listen and not just talk. You might be left amazed at what God has to tell you in return.

Prayer Guide:

- Thank God for His friendship.
- Express your desire for a sincerity of faith.
- Express your desire for personal spiritual growth, sensitivity to sin, and discipline to maintain a daily quiet time.
- Intercede for your spouse's spiritual growth, sensitivity to sin, and spiritual leadership.
- Pray for your children's spiritual growth and sensitivity to sin.
- Submit your day's activities to Him.

Memory Verse Goals:

- Read the verse of the week five times.
- Post the verse of the week in a prominent location.

Day 16

But go and learn what this means: 'I desire compassion, and not sacrifice,' for I did not come to call the righteous, but sinners." Matthew 9:13

Day's Reading: Matthew 9-10

Jesus quoted Hosea 6:6 both here and again in Matthew 12:7 — "For I delight in loyalty rather than sacrifice, and in the knowledge of God rather than burnt offerings." It stands to remind us that the heart of God desires our love and loyalty more than the observance of any rituals or religious customs. Just as the Pharisees had grown to forget this, so sometimes we also forget in the observance of our spiritual checklist:

- Daily Bible Study — check.
- Meal time prayer — check
- Memorize week's Bible verse — check
- Attend church on Sunday — check

Yes, while those are all good things, we would sometimes do well to remember the intent behind the words, "I desire compassion, and not sacrifice." With that said, it may be time we redesign our spiritual checklist.

Reflection:

- What activities or rituals do you have on your spiritual checklist that you often do just because you know it's the "Christian-thing" to do?
- How could you redesign your checklist to make it more merciful to you and others?

Prayer Guide:

- Thank God for His mercy.
- Request wisdom for you, your spouse, and your children regarding your time, talents, spiritual gifts, and finances.
- Pray for your immediate family members' and relatives' prayer requests/needs.
- Submit your day's activities to Him.

Memory Verse Goals:

- Look up any unfamiliar words or meanings found in the verse of the week.
- Pray and meditate on the verse of the week.

Day 17

When the Sabbath came, He began to teach in the synagogue; and the many listeners were astonished, saying, "Where did this man get these things, and what is this wisdom given to Him, and such miracles as these performed by His hands?
Mark 6:2

Day's Reading: Matthew 14, Mark 6, Luke 9:1-17

As I look at today's passages, I'm continually drawn to the story where Jesus walks on water. Did you notice any discrepancy between Matthew's account and Mark's account? That's right—Mark doesn't mention the part where Peter tries to walk on water to meet Jesus; he skips it completely. The question is why? If Mark is considered Peter's memoir, why did he choose to leave that part out? Was Peter embarrassed by the memory of his lack of faith? Did Mark think it distracted from the focus of Jesus as the miraculous Savior King? We will probably never know for certain, but it causes me to ponder—do I ever NOT tell about my faith OR my lack of faith stories because of my own embarrassment? Oh, how much more God might be able to use me if I opened my heart and left everything in His hands.

Reflection:

- Do you ever feel hindered from sharing your faith or lack of faith story because of the possibility of embarrassment? If so, what different outcome do you think could result if you chose to share instead?
- Which of today's miraculous stories of Jesus stood out the most in your mind? Why?

Prayer Guide:

- Petition for confidence to share your faith or lack of faith stories for the purpose of bringing others to Christ.
- Ask for an understanding of God's Word that leads to personal application.
- Pray for your friends' prayer requests/needs.
- Request wisdom regarding your children's friendships and influences.
- Submit your day's activities to Him.

Memory Verse Goals:

- Repeat the verse of the week phrase by phrase five times.

Day 18

Jesus said to them, "I am the bread of life; he who comes to Me will not hunger, and he who believes in Me will never thirst."
John 6:35

Day's Reading: John 6

Six months have passed since the disciples have shared the Good News about Jesus throughout Galilee. People are curious. News is spreading of his miracles. Many make the trip to come see for themselves if this Jesus really is all they say He is. Many are poor and quickly run out of provision for their families. Only 5 barley loaves and two fish can found in the crowd — the food of the poor.

Tradition stated that the Messiah would cause manna to fall from heaven as it did in Moses' time (Exodus 16:4, 5). Did the people make the miraculous connection between their traditional beliefs and this feeding of over 5,000 people? Possibly — which could be one reason why Jesus uses so many references here to being the bread of life. The only difference — anyone who eats of this bread (that is believes in Jesus) has eternal life. Jesus' bread would sustain them not only for a day but for eternity.

Reflection:

- How would you have responded if you had sat on the hill, receiving these words for the first time? Would you have been a verse 66 or a verse 69 statistic?
- What words seemed to stand out most to you today from this passage? Why?

Prayer Guide:

- Thank God for the blessing of your faith.

- Share with Him your heart—that you desire it to be filled with greater love and compassion for your children, your spouse, and those around you.
- Surrender your spouse's heart--that it would be filled with greater love and compassion for you and your children.
- Relinquish your children's hearts—that they would be filled with greater love and compassion for their siblings and others.
- Submit your day's activities to Him.

Memory Verse Goals:

- Say the verse of the week aloud twenty times in a row.

Day 19

"'This people honors Me with their lips, but their heart is far away from Me. But in vain do they worship Me, teaching as doctrines the precepts of men.'" Matthew 15:8-9

Day's Reading: Matthew 15, Mark 7

The story of the Gentile woman whose daughter was demon possessed has often intrigued me and baffled me. Why would Jesus respond to her in such a way that it appeared he was shoving her off? Well, as God would have it, nothing could have been further from the truth, but let's start at the beginning of the story to get a better understanding.

Jesus had just traveled to the region of Tyre and Sidon, about 50 miles from Capernaum, which is the farthest he is recorded to have traveled during his public ministry. Why had He traveled there? To get away from the crowds and their constant beckoning, to relax, and to bond with his disciples. Yet, this woman would not leave them alone. If I were Jesus at this point, I would have been totally annoyed because I had tried so hard to escape the constant requests for healing, yet all the while this woman wouldn't stop pestering. That said, unlike me, Jesus calmly responded, "Let the children be satisfied first, for it is not good to take the children's bread and throw it to the dogs." (Mark 7:27). His remark meant no harm--just a request for patience. My interpretation—"Woman, please. Let me spiritually feed my disciples first and then I will help you when we are done." Her reply? "I know you need to feed your disciples, but even little dogs consume children's scraps from the table." (my rough paraphrase). Meaning--"My Jesus, I know you are leading your disciples, but I'm desperate. I'll do anything because I know your food is the only kind I need." Jesus, recognizing her persistence as faith, heals her daughter that very hour. Conclusion? Sometimes persistence, however mundane, is the key to true faith. Keep pursuing Jesus; it's totally worth it.

Reflection:

- Which character in today's passage do you most relate to: The disciples who were left pondering? The Pharisees whose religion was more for show than a result of faith? Or the Gentile woman, whose persistence and faith led to the healing of her daughter? Why?
- How will the story of the Gentile woman's persistence change how you pursue Jesus in the future? What steps are you going to take to put that change into motion?

Prayer Guide:

- Thank God for the salvation of Gentiles and Jews.
- Pray for your and your spouse's safety, purity, and power to resist sexual and/or emotional temptation.
- Request help regarding your children's safety, wisdom, and purity.
- Pray for the safety and wisdom for the military and those you know in the military.
- Submit your day's activities to Him.

Memory Verse Goals:

- Review the verse of the week ten times in a row.
- Review Luke 2:52 (from week 1) one time.
- Review Matthew 5:16 (from week 2) two times.

Day 20

And He was saying to them all, "If anyone wishes to come after Me, he must deny himself, and take up his cross daily and follow Me." Luke 9:23

Day's Reading: Matthew 16, Mark 8, Luke 9:18-27

The stage is set. Jesus and the disciples have just arrived in Caesarea Philippi after some repeatedly stressful encounters with some Pharisees requesting signs to know who Jesus is. Currently known as Banias today, Caesarea Philippi was known for their local gods—idols carved into a nearby 100 foot rocky cliff next to the Jordan river.

I can almost see it—Jesus and His disciples sitting next to this rocky façade as He says, "Who do you say that I am?" (Matthew 16:15), and "...you are Peter, and upon this *rock* I will build My church..." (Matthew 16:18). Wow. Can you imagine? Next to these rocky gods, Christ led His disciples to a proclamation of the one true God and created His own rock solid foundation in Peter, a name both Peter and the church will never forget. Now it's your turn. You are at the edge of this rocky cliff—who do you say Jesus is? On which rock will you choose to stand?

Reflection:

- As followers of Jesus, we are to "take up our cross and follow Him." What is your cross? How have you taken up your cross to follow Jesus?
- In light of the setting, how does this story of Jesus' disciple proclaiming Christ's deity come to life for you?

Prayer Guide:

- Praise the Lord for Who He is.
- Pray for strength to take up whatever cross it is you must bear as a follower of Christ.
- Ask for opportunities and confidence to show your spouse respect, grace, and kindness every day.
- Intercede for your children — that they would develop a heart of compassion, service, and prayer.
- Plead with God on behalf of the poor, hungry, and persecuted.
- Dedicate to God personally known city, state, national, and international mission efforts.
- Submit your day's activities to Him.

Memory Verse Goals:

- Review the verse of the week three times in a row.
- Review Luke 2:52 (from week 1) and Matthew 5:16 (from week 2) one time.

Day 21

Sitting down, He called the twelve and said to them, "If anyone wants to be first, he shall be last of all and servant of all." Mark 9:35

Day's Reading: Matthew 17, Mark 9, Luke 9:28-62

From the time we are little, the American Dream is instilled in us. "You can do it! You can be anything you want to be! You can win! You're the best!" In fact, that dream has been so instilled within us that we are now living what many are calling the "Age of Entitlement" — the time where "I deserve it" and "I should be treated first" attitudes abound. It's infectious. It's debilitating. It's a lie.

Take a look a Mark 9:35 and you'll see it's true. To lead is to serve. Put that in the context of your life. To lead is to serve. To lead your children is to serve your children. To lead your Sunday School class is to serve your Sunday School class. To lead your employees is to serve your employees. To lead is to serve. That's definitely a different attitude than one of entitlement — one that can only be obtained when we lean on Jesus, the ultimate servant of all, to give us the strength and humility we need to serve.

Reflection:

- This "greatest of all" discussion paradoxically occurred soon after three of them saw the transfiguration of Jesus. Sometimes when we get closer to a source of power, we can get greedy. Whether it's a rise in job status, the forming of a friendship with someone of importance, or running in a race, the closer we get, the more we want what they have — to be the best. How should our attitude be different when we come in contact with these situations?

- What does "to lead is to serve" look like in your life? How might that view change how you pursue a certain aspect of your life?

Prayer Guide:

- Praise God for personal spiritual victories found in your life and those around you.
- Request a servant's heart.
- Relinquish to God each immediate family member's self-confidence and self-motivation to do and be what He wants them to be.
- Pray for your church and the leadership therein.
- Submit your day's activities to Him.

Memory Verse Goals:

- Review the verse of the week one time.
- Review Luke 2:52 (from week 1) and Matthew 5:16 (from week 2) one time.

Week 4

So Jesus was saying to those Jews who had believed
Him, "If you continue in My word, then you are
truly disciples of Mine; and you will know the truth, and the
truth will make you free." John 8:31-32

Day 22

"*Should you not also have had mercy on your fellow slave, in the same way that I had mercy on you?*" *Matthew 18:33*

Day's Reading: Matthew 18

We live in a prideful and an "I am better than you" world. Whether we like it or not, this sinful and selfish nature within us often carries over when we become Christians. The church is filled with prideful people. Yet Jesus, throughout the whole chapter, encourages just the opposite; he encourages humility. As Christians we need each other. We are a team— God's team. We need to be humble enough and forgiving enough to work together for God's glory because no one is perfect, and together we can accomplish so much more.

Reflection:

- When are you most often proud? What can you do to be more humble in that situation?
- Is there someone you need to forgive? If so, what can you do to make that happen today?

Prayer Guide:

- Pray for humility of heart.
- Share with Him your longing for a heart filled with worship.
- Request His leadership regarding your family, your family's activities, and your family's goals.
- Ask for discipline to accomplish your personal goals, Lord willing.
- Submit your day's activities to Him.

Memory Verse Goals:

- Read the verse of the week five times.
- Post the verse of the week in a prominent location.

Day 23

He who believes in Me, as the Scripture said, 'From his innermost being will flow rivers of living water.'" John 7:38

Day's Reading: John 7-8

It was Fall...the last day of the Feast of Tabernacles (the religious festival that was all about thanking God for His provisions and remembering Israelite history). For these seven days people built and lived in makeshift lean-to's made of branches and leaves to remember the days the Israelites wandered in the desert and had no permanent home. On each day of the feast, the people marched around the big altar of Jerusalem with palm branches in worship to God. On the last day, they marched around the altar seven times to honor the memory of the walls of Jericho. At the same time a priest would take a golden pitcher of water from the Pool of Siloam and pour it on the altar as an offering to God. It could have been at this very moment, when the priest was pouring the water on the altar, that Jesus cried out, "If anyone is thirsty, let him come to Me and drink. He who believes in Me, as the Scripture says, 'From his innermost being will flow rivers of living water'" (John 7:37-38). Imagine the shock. Imagine the awe. Imagine how these Jews might have felt upon hearing those words at that exact moment. Is this really the Christ?

Reflection:

- How does the possible setting of Jesus' words in chapter 7 change the impact of Christ's words for you?
- Chapter 8 talks about abiding in the Word or continually learning and obeying the Word. What do you do to continually abide in Christ each day? Be encouraged. By doing this study you are on the right track.

Prayer Guide:

- Make a commitment to abide in Him.
- Pray for a development of an eternal perspective in you and your family members.
- Request health and salvation for your family members.
- Ask for wisdom in teaching your children about loyalty and responsibility.
- Submit your day's activities to Him.

Memory Verse Goals:

- Look up any unfamiliar words or meanings found in the verse of the week.
- Pray and meditate on the verse of the week.

Day 24

"I am the good shepherd; the good shepherd lays down His life for the sheep. John 10:11

Day's Reading: John 9:1-10:21

In the Old Testament, when Moses asks God whom he should say sent Him, God replies "I AM WHO I AM...I AM has sent me to you" (Exodus 3:14). Meaning—God is the eternal one, the creator of all things, the covenantal God. Several times throughout John, Jesus proclaimed the very same words about Himself so that by the end it was abundantly clear—Jesus was claiming to be God! Take a look at some of these statements and you will see what I mean:

- "I am the bread of life." (John 6:35, 41, 48, 51)
- "I am the light of the world." (John 8:12)
- "... before Abraham was born, I AM." (John 8:58)
- "I am the door of the sheep." (John 10:7, 9)
- "I am the good shepherd." (John 10:11, 14)
- "I am the resurrection and the life." (John 11:25)
- "I am the way, the truth and the life." (John 14:6)
- "I am the true vine." (John 15:1, 5)

Reflection:

- Which "I AM" statement do you find most meaningful to you personally? Why?
- Imagine you had been the man in this passage who was born blind and made well by Jesus. How might you have responded to the Pharisees' perpetual questions?

Prayer Guide:

- Praise Jesus for being your "I AM."
- Defer to God the courage to speak with bold confidence about Jesus as the blind man did before the Pharisees.
- Ask for an understanding of God's Word that leads to personal application.
- Request spiritual, mental, and emotional health for you and your family members.
- Pray for your neighbors' prayer requests/needs.
- Submit your day's activities to Him.

Memory Verse Goals:

- Repeat the verse of the week phrase by phrase five times.

Day 25

And He was saying to them, "The harvest is plentiful, but the laborers are few; therefore beseech the Lord of the harvest to send out laborers into His harvest. Luke 10:2

Day's Reading: Luke 10-11, John 10:22-42

Have you ever read a passage of scripture only to read it again later and say, "I didn't realize that story was in there? That's exactly how I felt while reading Luke 10:1-12 today. I knew Jesus sent the twelve out to spread the Good News about Jesus (Luke 9:1-6), but I hadn't realized he sent out *70* others later on as well. Can you imagine the impact of 70 on-fire people for the Lord sharing the Good News in a concentrated area? And yes, as Jesus says, "the laborers are *few*" (personal emphasis added; Luke 10:2). Today there are approximately 300,000 Christian missionaries in the world. While that may sound like a lot, compared to a world population of 7 billion the workers are still indeed few. It sounds like our work is still set out before us — to pray for more workers. Could one of them be you?

Reflection:

- Did any of the passages you read today catch you by surprise? If so, which and why?
- What do you do to spread the Good News to the world around you?

Prayer Guide:

- Pray for laborers to spread the Good News.
- Request wisdom regarding your family's finances and discipline to use the money God's given you for His glory.

- Pray for the moral integrity of the next generation.
- Surrender to God your children's future mates.
- Submit your day's activities to Him.

Memory Verse Goals:

- Say the verse of the week aloud twenty times in a row.

Day 26

"And He said to His disciples, "For this reason I say to you, do not worry about your life, as to what you will eat; nor for your body, as to what you will put on. For life is more than food, and the body more than clothing." Luke 12:22-23

Day's Reading: Luke 12-13

Worry. It's infectious. It's overwhelming. It's debilitating. Even now, as I write these words I feel the effects of stress and worry in my life—tense shoulders, a kink in my neck, a twitching eye. Yes, worry can definitely debilitate. So why do we worry if we know it will do us no good? Do we still think we can actually do something God can't? Or, do we take on too much, thinking we can when God didn't design us to run 100 miles per hour all the time?

"For where your treasure is, there your heart will be also" (Luke 12:34). Where your thoughts are, where your time is, where your energy is spent, where your relationships develop, where your money goes, where your focus lies-- there your heart will be also. Have you ever read Luke 12:35-48 in light of Luke 12:22-34 (which comes right before it)? When looking at this passage more closely, I think it is no coincidence that the parable of the faithful servant follows the first passage because if we "[get] dressed in readiness, and *keep* [our] lamps lit [and] be like men who are waiting for their master" (Luke 12:35-36), our priorities would be in a much godlier order and a much less stressful order because both our heart and treasure will be in the same place, just as God designed it.

Reflection:

- Where are your thoughts, time, money, energy, relationships, and focus spent? If not on Jesus, why not and how could you change it to further glorify Him?

- Make a list of where you spend your time and how much time you spend doing each activity in a typical day. Consider also doing this with your money over a week or month. Do you see anything that you might need to adjust in light of God's priorities? If so, then bring it to Him and work with Him to come up with a plan of action to make the change.

Prayer Guide:

- Present to God things that have caused you worry or stress. Give your stress/worry to Jesus.
- Request physical strength and health for you, your spouse, and your children.
- Surrender to God your city, state, and national governments and the current issues therein.
- Pray for world leaders, events, and concerns.
- Submit your day's activities to Him.

Memory Verse Goals:

- Review the verse of the week ten times in a row.
- Review Luke 2:52 (from week 1) and Matthew 5:16 (from week 2) one time.
- Review Mark 8:34 (from week 3) two times.

Day 27

"For everyone who exalts himself will be humbled, and he who humbles himself will be exalted." Luke 14:11

Day's Reading: Luke 14-15

Pride is an over high opinion of oneself, and it's probably one of the sins I struggle with the most. In fact, I feel embarrassed to even admit it. For me, it's such a challenge to find a balance between the first definition of pride, the sinful, selfish kind of pride that Jesus talks about in Luke 14:11 and the third definition which is "a delight or satisfaction in one's own or another's achievements" similar to that which is expressed in 2 Corinthians 7:4 or 5:12 . As an occasional performing musician, I must take pride or have confidence in myself in order to do a good job, but not become so overly confident that I think more highly of myself than I ought. It is then that it becomes sin…and it is then that I am more likely to forget my words, the music, or become impersonal with my audience.

It's the same with life. We can be proud of our possessions, our jobs, our children, our spouses, or our situations to the point that it debilitates our effectiveness for the Lord or our humbleness to accept the Lord's grace. Ultimately, we must never forget to give credit where credit is due—to our God who has created all things and in whom all things are sustained (Colossians 1:16). He alone deserves the glory.

Reflection:

- In what areas of your life do you struggle with pride? How can you give God the glory in those situations?
- In the parable of the lost son who do you most relate to? Why?

Prayer Guide:

- Request a humble confidence in all you do.
- Ask for the Lord's blessing/enablement in your family's life roles.
- Pray for your family's energy, enthusiasm, and success in career settings.
- Surrender to God your children's education and those involved in their education.
- Submit your day's activities to Him.

Memory Verse Goals:

- Review the verse of the week three times in a row.
- Review Matthew 5:16 (from week 2)and Mark 8:34 (from week 3) one time.

Day 28

"He who is faithful in a very little thing is faithful also in much; and he who is unrighteous in a very little thing is unrighteous also in much." Luke 16:10

Day's Reading: Luke 16-17:10

The parable of the unjust steward has often baffled me because by all initial appearances it looks like the steward, being angry with his master, selfishly stole what was to be his master's money by discounting his master's debtors' bills. His hope--that doing so would provide him shelter later once unemployed. However, upon further research nothing could have been further from the truth. Stewards often received a commission from debts paid by charging interest on the debt. Instead of taking his master's money, he used wisdom to relinquish his own earnings in the immediate situation in hopes of a home in the future. Yes, the steward may have been angry with his master at first. Yes, he may have felt unjustified in the process. But, he did not let that stop him from using wisdom to prepare for the future and give back to others in the process.

Compare the above story to this—a man is poor and hungry. One passerby stops and tells the poor man he needs Jesus but then quickly continues on his way. Another man stops, and upon seeing that the poor man is hungry, takes him to a local restaurant and buys him a meal before telling him about Jesus. To which person is the poor man more likely to listen and potentially receive the Good News? The first one, who was all mouth and no action, or the second one who was willing to give of himself and his money to further reach the heart of the poor man? In the same way, if we are faithful to share our money and possessions wisely and unselfishly with others, non-Christians are more likely to receive us in the future and listen to us tell them about our forever home. "He who is faithful in a very little thing [money, possessions, etc.] is faithful also in much [spiritual matters and the Good News of Jesus]" (Luke 16:10, personal paraphrase added).

Reflection:

- What can you give to someone today that may open the door to a spiritual conversation in the future?
- What stood out to you most in the story about the steward? How will it change your actions in the future?

Prayer Guide:

- Express a desire for a wise and giving heart and hand.
- Request an opportunity to share some possessions or money to further spread the Good News.
- Ask for boldness and sensitivity to reach the lost and needy around you.
- Dedicate your church's ministries to Him.
- Pray for sensitivity to serve where needed in your community and/or church.
- Submit your day's activities to Him.

Memory Verse Goals:

- Review the verse of the week one time.
- Review Matthew 5:16 (from week 2) and Mark 8:34 (from week 3) one time.

Week 5

"If anyone serves Me, he must follow Me; and where I am, there My servant will be also; if anyone serves Me, the Father will honor him." John 12:26

Day 29

Jesus said to her, "I am the resurrection and the life; he who believes in Me will live even if he dies." John 11:25

Day's Reading: John 11

It seems like whenever discussions rise about Martha and Mary, Martha often gets a bad rap thanks to Luke 10:41-42. However, I love this passage because it lets Martha's faith shine through. Who comes to Jesus first? Martha. Who proclaims faith in Jesus first? Martha. Who draws her sister to Jesus? Martha. Yes, we may all have our distracted moments like Martha in Luke 10:41-42 where we lose our perspective and focus, but as Martha shows, it doesn't have to always be like that. Oh what an encouragement—especially for this often distracted mother of preschoolers.

Reflection:

- What encouraged you most from today's passage?
- Have you chosen to believe in Jesus as Martha did in verse 27? If so, whom can you go tell about what Jesus has done in your life?

Prayer Guide:

- Pray for an unwavering faith in Jesus as the Christ.
- Request an opportunity to share the Good News with another.
- Express your desire for personal spiritual growth, sensitivity to sin, and discipline to maintain a daily quiet time.
- Intercede for your spouse's spiritual growth, sensitivity to sin, and spiritual leadership.

- Pray for your children's spiritual growth and sensitivity to sin.
- Submit your day's activities to Him.

Memory Verse Goals:

- Read the verse of the week five times.
- Post the verse of the week in a prominent location.

Day 30

"I tell you, this man went to his house justified rather than the other; for everyone who exalts himself will be humbled, but he who humbles himself will be exalted." John 18:14

Day's Reading: Luke 17:11-18:14

I do not like conflict. Some people don't seem to mind it and even take it on as a challenge. But me — it stresses me out! I want to resolve the issue the best I can right away so I can move on. Otherwise I will stew over it and wrestle with it all night long night after night. However, sometimes a quick resolution is not always possible. I can think of one instance this year alone in which an individual retaliated against a decision I made, and the unresolved conflict from that decision continues to this day (now many months later). Even though I've tried my best to resolve the issue with the party involved, this woman continues to throw daggers my direction hurting me, my family, her, her family, and many of those in the same community in which we live. Sometimes I just want to roll back the curtain and let everyone know the injustice this person has caused, but that would only make the situation worse. Instead, I must remember just as Jesus revealed in the parable of the persistent widow that I must leave revenge to God because He knows all things and how the situation can best be resolved without causing more hurt. And sometimes, it's just nice to know that my heavenly Father is standing up for me so I don't have to. There's a special comfort and peace found only when I give an anxious heart to Jesus. Thank goodness our God is both a God of mercy and a God of justice. He is my resolve.

Reflection:

- Which attitude do you possess more often — the attitude of the Pharisee or the tax collector?

- Is there a situation in which you feel unjustified and need to give it to Jesus? If so, what?

Prayer Guide:

- Surrender any situation in which you may feel unjustified.
- Ask for a humble heart similar to the tax collector.
- Request wisdom for you, your spouse, and your children regarding your time, talents, spiritual gifts, and finances.
- Pray for your family's prayer requests/needs.
- Submit your day's activities to Him.

Memory Verse Goals:

- Look up any unfamiliar words or meanings found in the verse of the week.
- Pray and meditate on the verse of the week.

Day 31

For even the Son of Man did not come to be served, but to serve, and to give His life a ransom for many." Mark 10:45

Day's Reading: Matthew 19, Mark 10

Tension is growing. The discussion of controversial topics is on the rise. In fact, Jesus knows His time is short so He lets it all loose in preparation of His triumphal entry only days later. What are Jesus' thoughts on marriage? On money? On children? On the sick? In Jesus' day these topics were very controversial. Thus, Jesus' sermons on these topics were probably what eventually led the Pharisees to act on their plans to have Jesus killed.

Similar to Jesus' time, the topics of marriage, money, children and the sick continue to be controversial in the 21st century. Thus, it's no wonder divorce rates, credit card debt, abortion numbers, and child care attendance remain ever on the rise. While opinions of the sick may be a little better in today's society with interest in making things handicap accessible and medical clinics plentiful, our opinion of the homeless is much the same. For instance, what are your immediate thoughts when you see a homeless person on the side of the road? For many, the answer would probably be very similar to the crowd in the story of Bartimaeus (Mark 10:46-52). Yes, these topics are definitely still controversial. And a call for our response is much the same — will we side with Jesus and his desire for us to serve others, or will we side with our society and the desire to serve ourselves? The choice is never easy, and God is gracious no matter what, but as Jesus declares, "with God all things are possible" (Mark 10:27). So how, then, will you choose to live?

Reflection:

- Which of these stories hits closest to home for you? Why? What will you pray to do differently in the future as a result?
- If someone were to take a look at your checkbook or day planner, what would they see as your top priorities? Jesus? Others? Or yourself? How could you modify your finances to better glorify God?

Prayer Guide:

- Thank God for His grace and His power to make all things possible.
- Petition for a conviction of sin to the point of change.
- Ask for an understanding of God's Word that leads to personal application.
- Pray for your friends' prayer requests/needs.
- Request wisdom regarding your children's friendships and influences.
- Submit your day's activities to Him.

Memory Verse Goals:

- Repeat the verse of the week phrase by phrase five times.

Day 32

The crowds going ahead of Him, and those who followed, were
shouting, "Hosanna to the Son of David; blessed is He who
comes in the name of the Lord; Hosanna in the highest!"
Matthew 21:9

Day's Reading: Matthew 20-21

The time has come for Jesus to present himself as the
nation's Messiah. Jesus knows it. His followers know it.
There's excitement in the air. Expectation. Hope. Could
their dreams really be coming true in this man called Jesus?
A donkey and colt are retrieved from an owner who is most
likely a follower of Jesus to fulfill the prophecy of Zechariah
9:9. Garments are laid on both so Jesus can choose to sit on
that which he feels most comfortable. It's a humble
indication, this sitting on a donkey instead of a kingly horse.
The crowd that has followed him makes a big to-do about this
entry, laying down their garments before Jesus and waving
palm branches as they yell, "Hosanna!" which literally means
"save now!" Jesus' disciples and the crowd that has followed
him have set the stage—the Messiah is here! The only
problem is they had yet to realize what He was really there to
do.

Reflection:

- If you had been alive during Jesus' time, where do
  you think you might have been in the triumphal
  scene? One of Jesus' disciples? One of the
  multitudes? One of the Pharisees? One of the curious
  townspeople? Why?
- In explaining the story of the fig tree, Jesus said,
  "Whatever things you ask in prayer, believing, you

will receive" (Matthew 21:22). What do you need to ask Jesus today, believing it will be so?

Prayer Guide:

- Thank God for Jesus' coming as the Messiah.
- Express your need for a stronger faith in a given circumstance.
- Share with Him your heart—that you desire it to be filled with greater love and compassion for your children, your spouse, and those around you.
- Surrender your spouse's heart—that it would be filled with greater love and compassion for you and your children.
- Relinquish your children's hearts—that they would be filled with greater love and compassion for their siblings and others.
- Submit your day's activities to Him.

Memory Verse Goals:

- Say the verse of the week aloud twenty times in a row.

Day 33

...saying to them, "It is written, 'And My house shall be a house of prayer,' but you have made it a robbers' den."
Luke 19:46

Day's Reading: Luke 18:15-19:48

What do you do when you go to church? Do you attend a Bible study? Listen to a preacher? Sing songs of worship? While all that is well and good, and even biblically encouraged in other passages of scripture, I suppose the question I should really ask here is do you pray? I don't mean bow your head in the observance of a ritual. I mean do you really pray? Do you take that time to pray for your neighbors, your co-workers, your friends, the unreached around you, your church members, or the government? I am just as guilty as the next person when it comes to this, but did you hear Jesus' words? "My house is a house of prayer" (Luke 19:46). Is your church known as a "house of prayer"? Are you known as a person of prayer? If not, maybe it's time both our tables were overturned and our inner temples cleaned out to make room for what is more important — listening and talking to God.

Reflection:

- How important is prayer in your life? What could you rearrange in your life to make more time for prayer?
- What could you do to approach prayer with more sincerity while at church?

Prayer Guide:

- Express your desire to be sincere in prayer.

- Pray for your and your spouse's safety, purity, and power to resist sexual and/or emotional temptation.
- Request help regarding your children's safety, wisdom, and purity.
- Pray for the safety and wisdom for the military and those you know in the military.
- Submit your day's activities to Him.

Memory Verse Goals:

- Review the verse of the week ten times in a row.
- Review Matthew 5:16 (from week 2) and Mark 8:34 (from week 3) one time.
- Review John 8:31-32 (from week 4) two times.

Day 34

Whenever you stand praying, forgive, if you have anything against anyone, so that your Father who is in heaven will also forgive you your transgressions. But if you do not forgive, neither will your Father who is in heaven forgive your transgressions." Mark 11:25-26

Day's Reading: Mark 11, John 12

Ouch! I feel some toes being stepped on today. Do you? Forgiveness. It's an act of servanthood and humility to forgive someone. Forgiveness means to renounce anger or resentment that could result from an injustice and let it go. I don't know about you, but sometimes I really struggle with just letting it go. For me, it probably is one of the most challenging requests Jesus asks of me, especially when someone has intentionally done me wrong. Often I just want to be angry, get revenge, or whimper for pity from others rather than deal with the heart of the issue—my pride.

More often than not, what keeps us from forgiving another? Our pride. And pride has no place in heaven which is why Jesus said, "if you do not forgive, neither will your Father in heaven forgive your trespasses" (Mark 11:26). Why? Yes, it is hard. Yes, it is not very comfortable. But in forgiving we are learning to love like Jesus just a little more each time.

Reflection:

- Do you have someone in your life who has wronged you? Do you need to forgive them?
- What posture do you choose to be in when you pray? Jews generally stood when they prayed, covering their head in humility as they did so, while early Christians

often knelt in humble reverence when communicating with their Lord. Whatever posture you choose, does it involve a humble element? If not, consider trying a new posture when praying so as to give God all the glory and not yourself.

Prayer Guide:

- Request forgiveness and love for others despite hurt feelings.
- Thank God for Christ's forgiveness made complete on the cross.
- Ask for opportunities and confidence to show your spouse respect, grace, and kindness every day.
- Intercede for your children — that they would develop a heart of compassion, service, and prayer.
- Plead with God on behalf of the poor, hungry, and persecuted.
- Dedicate to God personally known city, state, national, and international mission efforts.
- Submit your day's activities to Him.

Memory Verse Goals:

- Review the verse of the week three times in a row.
- Review Mark 8:34b (from week 3) and John 8:31-32 (from week 4) one time.

Day 35

Jesus answered, "The foremost is, 'Hear, O Israel! The Lord our God is one Lord; and you shall love the Lord your God with all your heart, and with all your soul, and with all your mind, and with all your strength.' The second is this, 'You shall love your neighbor as yourself.' There is no other commandment greater than these." Mark 12:29-31

Day's Reading: Matthew 22, Mark 12

There are many laws in the Old Testament, many regulations that the Jews were to follow. Yet there were only ten commandments physically written by God (Exodus 20:1-17 and Deuteronomy 5:7-21). The lawyer knew this and wanted to know just how much of the law Jesus "really" knew. How did Jesus choose to respond? He chose to respond with the Jewish confession of faith, the Shema (Deuteronomy 6:4-9). The summary of the Shema (Deuteronomy 6:5), combined with His response in Matthew 22:39, generously encompassed the entire intent of the Ten Commandments and really all the law and prophets of the Old Testament.

The first four of the commandments are summarized in the Shema and Matthew 22:37 and Mark 12:30:

- "You shall have no other gods before me" (Exodus 20:3).
- "You shall not make for yourself an idol" (Exodus 20:4).
- "You shall not take the name of the Lord your God in vain" (Exodus 20:7).
- "Remember the Sabbath Day, to keep it holy" (Exodus 20:8)

The last six commandments are summarized in what Jesus terms as the second greatest commandment in Mathew 22:39 and Mark 12:31:

- "Honor your father and your mother" (Exodus 20:12).
- "You shall not murder" (Exodus 20:13).
- "You shall not commit adultery" (Exodus 20:14).
- "You shall not steal" (Exodus 20:15).
- "You shall not bear false witness" (Exodus 20:16).
- "You shall not covet" (Exodus 20:17).

Yes, there are "no other commandments greater than these" (Mark 12:31).

Reflection:

- How can you love the Lord your God today?
- How can you love your neighbor today?
- Do you have any idols you need to destroy or errands you need to save until Monday to keep the Sabbath day holy?

Prayer Guide:

- Pray for your neighbors and opportunities to reach out.
- Praise God for personal spiritual victories found in your life and those around you.
- Relinquish to God each immediate family member's self-confidence and self-motivation to do and be what He wants them to be.
- Pray for your church and the leadership therein.
- Submit your day's activities to Him.

Memory Verse Goals:

- Review the verse of the week one time.
- Review Luke 2:52 (from week 1), Mark 8:34 (from week 3) and John 8:31-34 (from week 4) one time.

Week 6

"Heaven and earth will pass away, but My words will not pass away." Luke 21:33

Day 36

"It will lead to an opportunity for your testimony. So make up your minds not to prepare beforehand to defend yourselves; for I will give you utterance and wisdom which none of your opponents will be able to resist or refute." Luke 21:13-15

Day's Reading: Matthew 23, Luke 20-21

No one ever really wishes to have pain, persecution, or affliction handed to them. Yet, when we think about some of the most amazing testimonies of our time, they have often come about as a result of trials. I've heard many a story where the death of someone dear, such as a small child or baby, combined with the God-given testimony of those remaining, draw many others to Christ. Onlookers find it hard to believe that anything or anyone could give peace in the midst of a horrible situation. Thus, they are mesmerized when they see it. I've heard of many cancer patients who have led their nurses to the Lord because of their behavior and personal testimony in the midst of what is often a very painful and trying time. And then there is me. I've thankfully not had to endure any of those things, and yet I plan what words I may say before I talk to anyone about Christ. Maybe I need to stop planning my words so much and praying more for opportunities to say them. Then God will truly get the glory because it will be His Words and not my own.

Reflection:

- Have you ever been in a trial or situation in which you had the opportunity to share about Jesus? If so, were you amazed at how God gave you the words to say?
- Who could you tell about what you are thankful for as a testimony to God's goodness?

Prayer Guide:

- Pray for opportunities to share your testimony.
- Intercede for those in the midst of trials — that peace and strength would be given to them and that their words will be a testimony of the Lord's handiwork to those around them.
- Share with Him your longing for a heart filled with worship.
- Request His leadership regarding your family, your family's activities, and your family's goals.
- Ask for discipline to accomplish your personal goals, Lord willing.
- Submit your day's activities to Him.

Memory Verse Goals:

- Read the verse of the week five times.
- Post the verse of the week in a prominent location.

Day 37

Then they will see the Son of Man coming in clouds with great power and glory. Mark 13:26

Day's Reading: Mark 13

Can you imagine what the people may have thought as Jesus spoke the words in today's passage? Most appropriately named the Olivet Discourse, Jesus was speaking these words while sitting on the Mount of Olives facing the temple. This temple was considered the most magnificent structure of its time with each stone weighing several tons. However, as Jesus spoke these words, the temple was not yet complete.

Work on the temple began in 20 B.C. under the direction of Herod the Great. Yet the placement of the 100 foot high marble stones and gold ornamentation with beautifully landscaped courtyards and walkways was not completed until 63 A.D. — over 30 years AFTER Jesus' death and resurrection. And this is the structure that Jesus and his followers were looking at as Jesus spoke these words: "Do you see these great buildings? Not one stone will be left upon another which will not be torn down" (Mark 13:2). I can just hear the people now: "You've got to be kidding, Jesus. Nothing could tear down these temple walls." Oh but they could. In fact, the temple was destroyed so well by the Romans in 70 A.D. that archeologists today still cannot determine the precise location of its origin.

Reflection:

- Read Mark 13:33 again. The great tribulation will most likely be just as shocking to us as the destruction of the temple in 70 A.D. was to the Jews living at the time. That said, what can you do or who can you tell about Jesus today so that you will be prepared for what could happen as soon as tomorrow?

- Do a search online to see if you can find a rendition of what the temple might have looked like during Jesus' time (search: "Herod's Temple A.D. 66"). Imagine how you might have felt if you were sitting on the Mount of Olives listening to Jesus' words as you looked at this magnificent structure. How might you have responded to Jesus' words spoken in this passage?

Prayer Guide:

- Request wisdom regarding life's priorities so as to be best prepared for Jesus' second coming.
- Pray for a development of an eternal perspective in you and your family members.
- Request health and salvation for your family members.
- Ask for wisdom in teaching your children about loyalty and responsibility.
- Submit your day's activities to Him.

Memory Verse Goals:

- Look up any unfamiliar words or meanings found in the verse of the week.
- Pray and meditate on the verse of the week.

Day 38

For this reason you also must be ready; for the Son of Man is coming at an hour when you do not think He will.
Matthew 24:44

Day's Reading: Matthew 24-25

The disciples thought that the destruction of the temple meant the end times. However, Jesus kept warning, "See to it that no one misleads you" (Matthew 24:4) because He knew they were having trouble distinguishing between the the the destruction of the temple and the end times. Now I'll be the first to say how little I know and understand about the end times, but this I do know — we have already seen:

- "wars and rumors of wars" (Matthew 24:6)
- "famines and earthquakes" (Matthew 24:7)
- "many false prophets" (Matthew 24:11)

And the fulfillment of the gospel being preached in all the world is so close that many mission efforts are predicting that its fulfillment could be accomplished in the next generation. If that is so, are you ready? Are those you know ready? Time is short. What are you going to do today to make the most of it?

Reflection:

- "For I was hungry, and you gave Me something to eat; I was thirsty, and you gave Me something to drink; I was a stranger, and you invited Me in; naked, and you clothed Me; I was sick, and you visited Me; I was in prison, and you came to Me" (Matthew 25:35-36). What are you doing to fulfill this verse?
- In many ways envisioning the second coming of Christ is unfathomable. Yet today, take some time to

close your eyes and imagine a little of what it might be like, and then praise God for His awesomeness and loving-kindness that is to come.

Prayer Guide:

- Express your desire to see the fulfillment of the gospel spread to all nations and ask how you can be involved.
- Praise God for His awesomeness and loving-kindness as portrayed in the prophecy of Christ's second coming.
- Ask for an understanding of God's Word that leads to personal application.
- Request spiritual, mental, and emotional health for you and your family members.
- Pray for your neighbors' prayer requests/needs.
- Submit your day's activities to Him.

Memory Verse Goals:

- Repeat the verse of the week phrase by phrase five times.

Day 39

And He was saying, "Abba! Father! All things are possible for You; remove this cup from Me; yet not what I will, but what You will." Mark 14:36

Day's Reading: Matthew 26, Mark 14

Pressures. Stress. Fears. Life has a way of throwing us curve balls sometimes. Yet no one reading today's passage will likely ever face the pressures Jesus was facing at this very moment. Oh how overwhelming it must have felt to be rejected by everyone around him (even if only for a time) — society, his friends, his disciples — even God the Father must separate himself for a time to fulfill the scriptures. We would do well to learn a couple of things from Jesus in this passage to apply the next time we face what we term as a great trial in our lives. Here are a few tips for such a time as this:

- Go to God. He's ultimately the only one who can truly help and who will always listen because He's your Abba Father...your Daddy. Curl up in his lap and tell him all about it. He's there for you.
- Then, don't just tell God about the situation; give it to Him and let Him do His will because in the end His will is always better than our own no matter how hard our problems look at the time.
- Confide in a few friends. Heaven knows, if Jesus needs a few companions, we need them ten times more. Don't try to go it alone. Ask for support.
- Know that it's okay to get frustrated. Just don't sin in your frustration. Did you notice the exclamation mark in Mark 14:42? Jesus is always calm in his responses except here. Likely he was feeling the pressure and it was starting to show, but in everything he did not sin. So be frustrated. It's totally understandable. Just do

your best to refrain from sinning in the process as Jesus did because God is still in control.

Reflection:

- What tips would you add to the above based on your analysis of these chapters?
- What trials are you currently facing? Are there any circumstances in which you could apply some of these trial tips?

Prayer Guide:

- Ask for wisdom regarding His will in the midst of your current trials.
- Thank Jesus for what He went through for you.
- Request wisdom regarding your family's finances and discipline to use the money God's given you for His glory.
- Pray for the moral integrity of the next generation.
- Surrender to God your children's future mates.
- Submit your day's activities to Him.

Memory Verse Goals:

- Say the verse of the week aloud twenty times in a row.

Day 40

A new commandment I give to you, that you love one
another, even as I have loved you, that you also love one
another. By this all men will know that you are My disciples,
if you have love for one another." John 13:34-35

Day's Reading: Luke 22, John 13

Sometimes I just don't want to be nice. I'd rather do my
own selfish thing and take care of my own selfish life. I know
it's not right, but I'm sure most of us would say we've felt
that way at one time or another because we're human and we
live in a fallen world.

So too, there were times when even Jesus was
disappointed by people or circumstances around him, but
unlike what often becomes our answer, Jesus always chose to
love. In fact, He loved people so much He died for them. Yes,
Jesus continued to love others and serve others throughout
His whole earthly ministry. He even loved Judas to the end,
washing his feet only hours before Judas betrayed Him. Talk
about an agape kind of love!

John 13:34 is a new commandment in that before Jesus the
law was always stated as "Love your neighbor as
YOURSELF" (Mark 12:31). Now Jesus alters that
commandment slightly so as to say "Love your neighbor
LIKE ME...like I've shown you." What an amazing example
Jesus set before us.

Reflection:

- How are Christians to be known? By their love. Are
  you known by your love or by something else?
- Have you ever washed someone else's feet, or have
  your feet ever been washed by someone? It is often a

humbling experience for both involved. Consider having a family foot washing one night after some barefoot playtime outdoors to share with your family what you have been learning about being known by your love.

Prayer Guide:

- Ask for a love for others, even in the tough situations.
- Request physical strength and health for you, your spouse, and your children.
- Surrender to God your city, state, and national governments and the current issues therein.
- Pray for world leaders, events, and concerns.
- Submit your day's activities to Him.

Memory Verse Goals:

- Review the verse of the week ten times in a row.
- Review Mark 8:34 (from week 3) and John 8:31-32 (from week 4) one time.
- Review John 12:26 (from week 5) two times.

Day 41

"This is My commandment, that you love one another, just as I have loved you." John 15:12

Day's Reading: John 14-17

It's the final moments before Jesus' betrayal. Jesus wants to be certain that the disciples have digested every bit of His wisdom possible. In addition, He prays over them and all who will come to believe in Him after His time on earth. He prays for me and for you. Jesus' command—" love one another, even as I have loved you" (John 13:34)—rings through even in this prayer. Pray for your fellow believers. They need it as much as you do.

Reflection:

- What does it mean to abide in something? What are you doing to abide in Jesus?
- Jesus laid down his life literally for our salvation. Is there an area you need to lay down in your life out of love for Him?

Prayer Guide:

- Intercede for fellow believers (boldness to share the gospel, sanctification in truth, etc.).
- Ask for the Lord's blessing/enablement in your family's life roles.
- Pray for your family's energy, enthusiasm, and success in career settings.
- Surrender to God your children's education and those involved in their education.
- Submit your day's activities to Him.

Memory Verse Goals:

- Review the verse of the week three times in a row.
- Review John 8:31-32 (from week 4) and John 12:26 (from week 5) one time.

Day 42

About the ninth hour Jesus cried out with a loud voice, saying, "Eli, Eli, lama sabachthani?" that is, "My God, My God, why have You forsaken Me?" Matthew 27:46

Day's Reading: Matthew 27, Mark 15

Oh how I cringe nearly every time I read this passage. Jesus is on the cross – in pain and alone. Yet in the midst of all of this He clings to what He knows – Psalm 22. This cry, this desperate cry, is not really a cry of abandonment at all but rather a reference to something far greater – the posterity of the Messiah – the posterity of Jesus. In Jesus' time, people would make reference to a Bible passage by quoting the first verse of the passage which is exactly what Jesus did here during his final moments on the cross. Read Psalm 22 for yourself and glory in the fact that "[Jesus] has done this" (Psalm 22:31).

Reflection:

- The people were persuaded by the chief priests to release Barabas instead of Jesus. Has there ever been a time you were persuaded by others to do or represent something you knew was not right? How can you guard against that in the future?
- The only man in the entire book of Mark to proclaim Jesus as the Son of God was the centurion in Mark 15:39. This Roman captain was probably the most unlikely person anyone would have expected to accept Jesus as Lord but he did. Is there someone in your life who is a lost cause for Jesus? If so, don't give up hope. Pray. If the centurion's heart can be turned, that person's heart can be turned too.

Prayer Guide:

- Praise God for sending His Son to save the world...to save you.
- Ask for boldness and sensitivity to reach the lost and needy around you.
- Dedicate your church's ministries to Him.
- Pray for sensitivity to serve where needed in your community and/or church.
- Submit your day's activities to Him.

Memory Verse Goals:

- Review the verse of the week one time.
- Review Matthew 5:16 (from week 2), John 8:31-32 (from week 4), and John 12:26 (from week 5) one time.

Week 7

"*Therefore repent and return, so that your sins may be wiped away, in order that times of refreshing may come from the presence of the Lord.*" Acts 3:19

Day 43

And Jesus, crying out with a loud voice, said, "Father, into Your hands I commit My spirit." Having said this, He breathed His last. Luke 23:46

Day's Reading: Luke 23, John 18-19

Wow. What a powerful verse. I mean, who else can control His last breath but God? No wonder the centurion proclaimed Christ as Lord. Yet, who didn't? Do you ever find it interesting WHOM Christ uses to proclaim His glory? Take this centurion for instance. Most likely his only encounter with Jesus was at the cross where the disciples, who were with him every day, hid. Or take Joseph and Nicodemus, two members of the Jewish council. Although previously secret followers of Christ, they risk ridicule and public rejection by burying Jesus' body after His death. They considered the cause worth it. And the disciples? They hid. Yes, we may not be strong or outgoing all the time, but God can still use us when we are. Are you willing?

Reflection:

- What is truth? Have you ever asked yourself that question? Just as Pilate wondered, how do you know what is truth?
- You have probably heard it said many times that the Bible says to "turn the other cheek" when faced with opposition (Matthew 5:39), and while Jesus did this when faced with physical violence in these verses, I find it interesting that He still stood up for himself in John 18:23. Why do you think he did this?

Prayer Guide:

- Praise God for His mighty power even in Jesus' last breath.
- Request an ever increasing understanding of the truth.
- Express your desire for personal spiritual growth, sensitivity to sin, and discipline to maintain a daily quiet time.
- Intercede for your spouse's spiritual growth, sensitivity to sin, and spiritual leadership.
- Pray for your children's spiritual growth and sensitivity to sin.
- Submit your day's activities to Him.

Memory Verse Goals:

- Read the verse of the week five times.
- Post the verse of the week in a prominent location.

Day 44

And Jesus came up and spoke to them, saying, "All authority has been given to Me in heaven and on earth. Go therefore and make disciples of all the nations, baptizing them in the name of the Father and the Son and the Holy Spirit, teaching them to observe all that I commanded you; and lo, I am with you always, even to the end of the age." Matthew 28:18-20

Day's Reading: Matthew 28, Mark 16

Commonly known as the Great Commission, this call to action is found in all four gospels (Matthew 28:18-20, Mark 16:15, Luke 24:47, John 20:21), making it some of the most important words Jesus ever spoke. Do you ever wonder what you should be doing for Christ? This is it. We should be glorifying Him in all we do and telling others about Him along the way, but even more we should be "making disciples." Making disciples entails a lot more than a onetime conversion encounter. It involves walking alongside another and guiding them in the teachings of Jesus so that they may be a strong enough Christian to stand on their own and in turn tell others about Jesus' teaching. While time really isn't the point, I've often heard it said that making a disciple usually takes a minimum of two years. If we were to take this one step further, Jesus spent three years training His disciples which is probably a good rule of thumb to follow. All that to say, this call to make disciples is no short-term project; it's a lifestyle.

Reflection:

- How do/can you make disciples in your own life? Can you teach a Sunday school class at church or a Bible study in your home? Or how about a study group in the lunch room at work?

- Is there someone you can personally share Christ with and/or mentor in the ways of Christ?

Prayer Guide:

- Pray that the gospel will continue to spread to all nations.
- Ask for opportunities, wisdom, and courage to disciple others in Christ.
- Request wisdom for you, your spouse, and your children regarding your time, talents, spiritual gifts, and finances.
- Pray for your family's prayer requests/needs.
- Submit your day's activities to Him.

Memory Verse Goals:

- Look up any unfamiliar words or meanings found in the verse of the week.
- Pray and meditate on the verse of the week.

Day 45

So Jesus said to them again, "Peace be with you; as the Father
has sent Me, I also send you." John 20:21

Day's Reading: Luke 24, John 20-21

If you had the chance to go out to lunch with anyone in
the world, living or dead, whom would you choose? If that
question were asked of me, I might choose Mary Magdalene.
I mean she must have been one amazing woman. In her
lifetime she wrestled with demons (Luke 8:2) until she met
Jesus and stayed by His side even while He was crucified
(Matthew 27:56, Mark 15:40, John 19:25), and buried (Mark
15:47, Matthew 27:61, Matthew 28:1, Mark 16:1). And whom
does Jesus appear to first after His resurrection? None other
than Mary Magdalene (Luke 24:10, Mark 16:9). Can you
imagine what stories she would have to tell? And what love
for Jesus would flow from her heart? Oh to be around a
person like that—I think it would be the spiritual retreat of a
lifetime.

Reflection:

- If you could go to lunch with any person mentioned in
  the four gospels besides Jesus, whom would you
  choose? Why?
- In the Bible, the number three represents permanence,
  completeness, and something of real substance. Prior
  to Jesus' death, Peter denies Christ three times
  signifying a permanent denial of Jesus. Thus, how
  fitting that Jesus gives Peter three times to restore his
  belief in Him—restoring permanence to His faith.
  Have you ever denied your faith? Isn't it good to
  know doubt doesn't have to be permanent? He can
  restore you too, just like He did Peter.

Prayer Guide:

- Praise Him for His resurrection.
- Seek a restoration of faith.
- Ask for an understanding of God's Word that leads to personal application.
- Pray for your friends' prayer requests/needs.
- Request wisdom regarding your children's friendships and influences.
- Submit your day's activities to Him.

Memory Verse Goals:

- Repeat the verse of the week phrase by phrase five times.

Day 46

"But you will receive power when the Holy Spirit has come upon you; and you shall be My witnesses both in Jerusalem, and in all Judea and Samaria, and even to the remotest part of the earth." Acts 1:8

Day's Reading: Acts 1-3

The Great Commission, mentioned here in Acts 1:8 as well as the conclusion of each of the gospels, is the binding feature that connects this only book of New Testament history with its predecessor, the book of Luke. It also serves as an outline to this book that shares the 30 year wild-fire like expansion of the gospel from Jerusalem to Rome. Acts 1:1 - 6:7 focuses on the witness of the Good News in Jerusalem and Judea. Acts 6:8 - 9:31 focuses on the witness of the Good News in Judea and Samaria. And, Acts 9:32 - 28:31 focuses on the witness of the Good News to Rome and the ends of the earth.

Luke, "the beloved physician" of Paul (Colossians 4:14), actually met Paul in Troas (Acts 16:8, 10) where he joined Paul's missionary team and took care of Paul until Paul's death in Rome (2 Timothy 4:11). The book of Acts is assumed to have been written sometime between Paul's house arrest in 60 A.D. and the persecution of Roman Christians by Nero in 64 A.D. since there is no mention of this event in the book of Luke. In summary, Acts is the story of how the indwelling of the Holy Spirit changed the world forever.

Reflection:

- Review Acts 2:40-47. What are some key characteristics of a growing church?

- How could you implement some of these characteristics in your own church life for the purpose of spreading the Good News?

Prayer Guide:

- Thank God for the Holy Spirit.
- Pray for the spread of the gospel to the ends of the earth.
- Share with Him your heart — that you desire it to be filled with greater love and compassion for your children, your spouse, and those around you.
- Surrender your spouse's heart--that it would be filled with greater love and compassion for you and your children.
- Relinquish your children's hearts — that they would be filled with greater love and compassion for their siblings and others.
- Submit your day's activities to Him.

Memory Verse Goals:

- Say the verse of the week aloud twenty times in a row.

Day 47

So they went on their way from the presence of
the Council, rejoicing that they had been considered worthy to
suffer shame for His name. Acts 5:41

Day's Reading: Acts 4-6

I don't know about you, but I'm not sure my initial
response would be to feel honored for being persecuted for
Jesus. Frustration? Maybe. Hurt? Definitely. But honor?
Probably not. Yet that is exactly how the disciples and even
Paul felt when persecuted for Jesus' name. And rightly so
because this persecution of believers is what eventually
caused New Testament Christians to spread throughout the
world thereby spreading the Good News to all creation (Acts
8:1).

Reflection:

- Can you think of a time when life was getting you
  down but later, as a result of that experience or hurt,
  you were able to do, go, or serve someone as a result?
  God is good and He can turn anything into something
  for His glory and His good. Talk about encouraging!
  So, next time you feel life getting you down, pray God
  will use that experience for His glory. Undoubtedly, I
  imagine He will.
- Read the prayer in Acts 4:25-30 as part of your prayer
  to Jesus today. May we have the boldness to be a
  witness for Jesus in our communities as the disciples
  did.

Prayer Guide:

- Thank God for the times He has turned your life's sour lemons into lemonade.
- Ask for boldness to share the Good New with others.
- Pray for your and your spouse's safety, purity, and power to resist sexual and/or emotional temptation.
- Request help regarding your children's safety, wisdom, and purity.
- Pray for the safety and wisdom for the military and those you know in the military.
- Submit your day's activities to Him.

Memory Verse Goals:

- Review the verse of the week ten times in a row.
- Review John 8:31-32 (from week 4) and John 12:26 (from week 5) one time.
- Review Luke 21:33 (from week 6) two times.

Day 48

And Philip said, "If you believe with all your heart, you may."
And he answered and said, "I believe that Jesus Christ is the
Son of God." Acts 8:37

Day's Reading: Acts 7-8

The story of the sorcerer's confession breaks my heart —
not just because he was insincere but because I can think of
countless other "Christians" in our churches today who do
the same thing Simon did — profess a belief in the Christian
faith from all outward appearances but not from a sincerity of
heart. See, Simon was motivated not by God but by attention,
authority, and wealth — what he thought he could get out of
his association with Jesus. How many "Christians" in our
churches today do the same thing? They say one thing with
their mouth but don't pray to God for forgiveness or believe
with all their heart that Jesus really is the Son of God as the
Ethiopian did. How I pray that your belief in Jesus is more
like that of the Ethiopian — sincere, humble, and heartfelt.

Reflection:

- Is your belief in Jesus sincere? If so, how is your faith
  lived out differently from those who are just putting
  on an act?
- If you are a true Christian, have you been baptized as
  a testimony to others about your faith? If not, "what
  hinders [you] from being baptized?" (Acts 8:36)

Prayer Guide:

- Request mercy for the insincere Christians in your
  community.
- Express your desire for a sincerity of faith.

- Ask for opportunities and confidence to show your spouse respect, grace, and kindness every day.
- Intercede for your children—that they would develop a heart of compassion, service, and prayer.
- Plead with God on behalf of the poor, hungry, and persecuted.
- Dedicate to God personally known city, state, national, and international mission efforts.
- Submit your day's activities to Him.

Memory Verse Goals:

- Review the verse of the week three times in a row.
- Review John 12:26 (from week 5) and Luke 21:33 (from week 6) one time.

Day 49

Opening his mouth, Peter said: "I most certainly understand now that God is not one to show partiality, but in every nation the man who fears Him and does what is right is welcome to Him. Acts 10:34-35

Day's Reading: Acts 9-10

Do you have prejudices? Okay, maybe you would say no from the modern use of that word but really think about it. If you were at church or a grocery store and saw someone with a rugged backpack on or lots of tattoos and a Mohawk, would you behave differently around them or at least have negative thoughts concerning their appearance? I would venture to think that whether we mean to or not, most of us are at least a little prejudiced in our hearts. Peter was facing this same issue in his heart regarding Cornelius and the Gentiles. What is even more interesting is to see God's work already in Peter's life regarding prejudice because Peter was staying with a tanner—a man of an undesirable and dirty trade at the time. After all, he dealt with dead animals and would have often been declared unclean for doing so. However, Gentiles were considered even worse at the time; many believed they ranked lower than dogs and were Satan's workers or hell's fire stokers. All that to say, this is truly an amazing story because it proves God loves everyone no matter the race or the past. Thank goodness.

Reflection:

- Have you ever displayed a prejudice against someone? Is there some way you could make it right?
- Or, is there a prejudice you could do something to begin overcoming? For instance, if you show prejudice to the homeless, could you take some sack

lunches to a few and spend an afternoon with them so that you could start to understand them better and thereby begin to minimize your prejudice by replacing it with Christ's love?

Prayer Guide:

- Praise God for personal spiritual victories found in your life and those around you.
- Thank God He is not prejudiced.
- Ask for the removal of prejudice in your own life and the filling of Jesus' love.
- Relinquish to God each immediate family member's self-confidence and self-motivation to do and be what He wants them to be.
- Pray for your church and the leadership therein.
- Submit your day's activities to Him.

Memory Verse Goals:

- Review the verse of the week one time.
- Review Mark 8:34 (from week 3), John 12:26 (from week 5) and Luke 21:33 (from week 6) one time.

Week 8

But the wisdom from above is first pure,
then peaceable, gentle, reasonable, full of mercy and good
fruits, unwavering, without hypocrisy.   James 3:17

Day 50

And when he had found him, he brought him to Antioch. And
for an entire year they met with the church and taught
considerable numbers; and the disciples were first
called Christians in Antioch. Acts 11:26

Day's Reading: Acts 11-12

Christian. We often take that label for granted in the
modern culture of Christian music, Christian apparel, and
even Christian nations, yet followers of Christ were not
always called Christians. Sometimes they were called of "the
Way" (Acts 9:2). Other times they were called the "tribe of
Christ." But originally "Christian" was a nickname given by
non-believers to mock believers of Christ. It wasn't until this
encounter in Antioch that believers embraced the name
"Christian."

Nowadays Christians often encounter another problem —
the pop culture "Christian." The term "Christian" is now
often associated with anything that is good or noble not just
those who worship Christ. In America especially many call
themselves "Christians" just because they live in what they
think is a Christian nation or because they think they are
good so they must be a Christian.

This pop view of Christianity has in turn created a
new challenge for the true believer — how to be a witness to
others in a pop Christian society so that non-believers
understand the difference between a pop culture Christian
and a true believing Christian. Who knows — maybe we will
eventually have to take on another mocking name such as
"Bible-thumpers" or "holy rollers," but if we do, I pray it's
because non-believers see the true love of Jesus in us shining
through, not because we are trying to be "holier than thou,"

which is a turn-off for nearly everyone, no matter what the nickname.

Reflection:

- If true Christians today were given a new nickname what would you like it to be?
- What are some ways in which Christians today can combat or demonstrate the difference in their faith between a pop culture Christian and a true worshipper of Christ?

Prayer Guide:

- Express your desire for a sincerity of faith.
- Request boldness to share Jesus with others.
- Share with Him your longing for a heart filled with worship.
- Request His leadership regarding your family, your family's activities, and your family's goals.
- Ask for discipline to accomplish your personal goals, Lord willing.
- Submit your day's activities to Him.

Memory Verse Goals:

- Read the verse of the week five times.
- Post the verse of the week in a prominent location.

Day 51

And the disciples were continually filled with joy and with the Holy Spirit. Acts 13:52

Day's Reading: Acts 13-14

Has anyone in your church ever left for the "mission field?" If so, did you or leaders in your church fast, pray, and/or lay hands on him/her before sending them off? I've been to a few commissioning services in my day and often I will see one or two of those practices engaged in but never, at least to my knowledge, fasting. Yet that is exactly what leaders of the early church did when sending new ministers out into the field — they fasted and prayed (Acts 13:3, 14:23). Fasting was an outward expression of sincere devotion and focus on the Lord. It was considered an act of extreme devotion to God, heart, mind, body and soul. Jesus fasted 40 days in the wilderness, and He even talked about the importance of its use throughout His ministry (Matthew 17:20-21). Yet for many of us (myself included), this spiritual discipline is often ignored. I wonder how much more our lives and/or the lives of those around us would be impacted for the Lord should we choose to embrace this discipline. Hmm...might be worth a try just to find out!

Reflection:

- Why do you think fasting is no longer encouraged in many Christian circles today?
- Do you think fasting should be something incorporated as a part of living out your faith? Why or why not?

Prayer Guide:

- Express your desire for a sincerity of faith.

- Ask to be filled with joy in the Holy Spirit as were Paul and the disciples.
- Pray for a development of an eternal perspective in you and your family members.
- Request health and salvation for your family members.
- Ask for wisdom in teaching your children about loyalty and responsibility.
- Submit your day's activities to Him.

Memory Verse Goals:

- Look up any unfamiliar words or meanings found in the verse of the week.
- Pray and meditate on the verse of the week.

Day 52

Submit therefore to God. Resist the devil and he will flee from you. Draw near to God and He will draw near to you. Cleanse your hands, you sinners; and purify your hearts, you double-minded. James 4:7-8

Day's Reading: James 1-5

James — it's undeniably one of my favorite books in the Bible. Why? I'm a how-to checklist kind of person and James is a how-to checklist kind of book. In fact, it's the only proverbial-like book in the New Testament. As commonly believed, the book of James was written by James, the half-brother of Jesus, who became a believer of Jesus' resurrection after Jesus' ascension and eventually took over the role of leadership in the Jerusalem church after Peter's release from prison (Acts 12:5-23). Growing up as a devout Jew, James takes into consideration that his readers are knowledgeable in Jewish ways even if they are now Christians, and he encourages Jewish believers to live out their new found faith so that others can see the difference Jesus can make. James' basic motto: "Believe in Him. Live for Him. Be Him."

Reflection:

- How can you further live your life to better reflect Jesus?
- James puts emphasis on equality in Christ. Is there someone to whom you show favoritism? Or partiality? What can you do differently so as to love them as Jesus would?

Prayer Guide:

- Plead with God on behalf of the poor, hungry, and persecuted.
- Request kindness for everyone you may come in contact with today.
- Ask for an understanding of God's Word that leads to personal application.
- Request spiritual, mental, and emotional health for you and your family members.
- Pray for your neighbors' prayer requests/needs.
- Submit your day's activities to Him.

Memory Verse Goals:

- Repeat the verse of the week phrase by phrase five times.

Day 53

"But we believe that we are saved through the grace of the Lord Jesus, in the same way as they also are." Acts 15:11

Day's Reading: Acts 15-16

How interesting it would have been to have lived during this time when the church was just learning what it meant to live and breathe as Christians. Should they circumcise? Should they not? Should there be other laws they should still try to abide by, or does the law matter anymore? Sounds like a struggle that we still wrestle with in a similar manner today. What should we be doing with our lives as a result of our faith in Jesus? Maybe that's why later in the Bible Paul writes "...work out your salvation with fear and trembling; for it is God who is at work in you, both to will and to work for *His* good pleasure" (Philippians 2:12-13).

Reflection:

- What outward signs or actions do you expect to see or not see among Christians today? Why? Are they biblically based expectations or are they culturally based expectations?
- Sometimes it is very hard to let go of beliefs of the past such as those from a previous belief system or those instilled in us growing up. Even the Christian Pharisees of the early church had this problem. When encountering contrasting beliefs among Christians, according to this passage who or what can we turn to in order to determine the truth?

Prayer Guide:

- Express your desire for a pure faith.

- Ask for wisdom to distinguish the difference between cultural beliefs and biblical beliefs.
- Request wisdom regarding your family's finances and discipline to use the money God's given you for His glory.
- Pray for the moral integrity of the next generation.
- Surrender to God your children's future mates.
- Submit your day's activities to Him.

Memory Verse Goals:

- Say the verse of the week aloud twenty times in a row.

Day 54

I have been crucified with Christ; and it is no longer I who live, but Christ lives in me; and the life which I now live in the flesh I live by faith in the Son of God, who loved me and gave Himself up for me. Galatians 2:20

Day's Reading: Galatians 1-3

How are you saved? By works? By faith? That was the big question Paul was trying to answer in the book of Galatians. False teachers had come to Galatia claiming salvation was by "works of the law," but Paul lovingly wrote back, "NO! Salvation is by faith alone."

We still struggle with this question in our current culture, if not as a denomination then as individuals. How often do you hear "Sure, I'm a Christian. Sure, I'll go to heaven. I'm a good person." But in reality, "good" really has nothing to do with it. Faith alone is the answer.

Reflection:

- What other scriptures can you think of off the top of your head that support salvation through faith alone?
- How do you distinguish faith and works in your life so that others know salvation is through faith alone?

Prayer Guide:

- Thank God for His grace.
- Ask for humility of mind in all you do so as not to forget that it is only through the grace of Jesus we are saved and not our works.
- Request physical strength and health for you, your spouse, and your children.

- Surrender to God your city, state, and national governments and the current issues therein.
- Pray for world leaders, events, and concerns.
- Submit your day's activities to Him.

Memory Verse Goals:

- Review the verse of the week ten times in a row.
- Review John 12:26 (from week 5) and Luke 21:33 (from week 6) one time.
- Review Acts 3:19 (from week 7) two times.

Day 55

Let us not lose heart in doing good, for in due time we will reap if we do not grow weary. Galatians 6:9

Day's Reading: Galatians 4-6

I don't know about you, but for me some days are tiring. I get tired of doing the dishes. I get tired of cooking every meal. I get tired of changing diapers and wiping snotty noses. Sometimes I just wish there was a mommy retreat where I could escape to rejuvenate. Don't get me wrong. I love my family very much. Just sometimes, in the mundane activities of life, it becomes challenging to keep doing good over and over. Yet that is exactly what God wants from us — to do good over and over for family, friends, neighbors, strangers, Christians and non-Christians alike. Why? Well, have you ever offered an incentive for your children so they will make the right choice? Christ has actually done the same for us. He wants us to do good to others so that His love shines through and draws others closer to Him and to help us do good, He has promised us an eternal reward (Revelation 22:12). So, next time you start to feel worn down from doing good, take heart — the reward will be worth it in the end.

Reflection:

- What are some ways you could show love to your fellow Christians this week?
- What are some "good" things that you do that you need to pray to God to help you to continue to do with a good attitude?

Prayer Guide:

- Request perseverance in doing good.

~ 126 ~

- Ask for the Lord's blessing/enablement in your family's life roles.
- Pray for your family's energy, enthusiasm, and success in career settings.
- Surrender to God your children's education and those involved in their education.
- Submit your day's activities to Him.

Memory Verse Goals:

- Review the verse of the week three times in a row.
- Review Luke 21:33 (from week 6) and Acts 3:19 (from week 7) one time.

Day 56

And He made from one man every nation of mankind to live on all the face of the earth, having determined their appointed times and the boundaries of their habitation, that they would seek God, if perhaps they might grope for Him and find Him, though He is not far from each one of us. Acts 17:26-27

Day's Reading: Acts 17-18:18

How amazing is our creator that He would make us with an innate desire to worship Him. How amazing...and how deceptive. Oh yes, how we deceive ourselves into thinking it is something else. A desire for more assurance or "likes" from friends. A desire for the latest tech gadget or a bigger home. A desire for our husbands to love us a certain way. We fill our lives with stuff and our hearts with other hopeful pleasures, not realizing that our true desire is to love and know Jesus more. How much time, energy, and money we'd save if we truly let that realization sink in—that it's really God we want, not the stuff. Maybe the next time we are desiring something of this world we should first spend some time with Jesus and make sure that it's not spending time with Him we really desire instead.

Reflection:

- How have you seen these verses played out in your own life?
- What is one thing you could do today to worship Jesus?

Prayer Guide:

- Share words of adoration and praise to the Creator.
- Express a desire for heavenly pleasures over earthly.

- Ask for boldness and sensitivity to reach the lost and needy around you.
- Dedicate your church's ministries to Him.
- Pray for sensitivity to serve where needed in your community and/or church.
- Submit your day's activities to Him.

Memory Verse Goals:

- Review the verse of the week one time.
- Review John 8:31-32 (from week 4), Luke 21:33 (from week 6) and Acts 3:19 (from week 7) one time.

Week 9

No temptation has overtaken you but such as is common to man; and God is faithful, who will not allow you to be tempted beyond what you are able, but with the temptation will provide the way of escape also, so that you will be able to endure it.   1 Corinthians 10:13

Day 57

Rejoice always; pray without ceasing; in everything give thanks; for this is God's will for you in Christ Jesus. Do not quench the Spirit; do not despise prophetic utterances. But examine everything carefully; hold fast to that which is good; abstain from every form of evil. 1 Thessalonians 5:16-22

Day's Reading: 1 Thessalonians 1-5, 2 Thessalonians 1-3

Do you want to know what a Christian's life should look like? Then Thessalonians is a good place to start. The Thessalonians were new Christians. They were unsure of what a growing faith looked like. They were trying their best to live for Jesus despite persecution, and Paul was very excited to encourage them to be strong in the Lord despite their situation. In fact, he even sent Timothy back to Thessalonica to check on the new converts. These letters are a result of their questions.

Reflection:

- Read 1 Thessalonians 5:16-22 again. Make it a guide to your prayers today. Take time to rejoice in whatever circumstances you are in, to give thanks in those circumstances, to pray for the action of the Holy Spirit, and so on.
- If you had a spiritual guide like Paul to whom you could ask any question and he would guide you with the correct answer, what would you ask?

Prayer Guide:

- See the first reflection above.

- Express your desire for personal spiritual growth, sensitivity to sin, and discipline to maintain a daily quiet time.
- Intercede for your spouse's spiritual growth, sensitivity to sin, and spiritual leadership.
- Pray for your children's spiritual growth and sensitivity to sin.
- Submit your day's activities to Him.

Memory Verse Goals:

- Read the verse of the week five times.
- Post the verse of the week in a prominent location.

Day 58

This took place for two years, so that all who lived in Asia heard the word of the Lord, both Jews and Greeks. Acts 19:10

Day's Reading: Acts 18:19-19:41

Have you ever heard the analogy that if you reach two people for Christ and they each reach two people and they each reach two people and so on that the world could be radically transformed within a couple of years? Well, that almost sounds like what happened with Paul and the school of Tyrannus.   They were not only daily growing in the Word but also sharing with others everything they were learning (Acts 19:10). As a result, the truth spread like wildfire. It is another example of James 1:22 in action. Being a true believer involves more than just a "quiet time" or church attendance; it involves the spreading of the good news of Jesus — getting out there and making a difference.

Reflection:

- What two people could you share the gospel with this week?
- Are you taking time to both receive the Word and share the Word daily?

Prayer Guide:

- Ask for boldness to share the truth with others.
- Pray for softened hearts willing to be changed by the gospel.
- Express a commitment to spending personal time growing in the Word.

- Request wisdom for you, your spouse, and your children regarding your time, talents, spiritual gifts, and finances.
- Pray for your family's prayer requests/needs.
- Submit your day's activities to Him.

Memory Verse Goals:

- Look up any unfamiliar words or meanings found in the verse of the week.
- Pray and meditate on the verse of the week.

Day 59

For it is written, "I will destroy the wisdom of the wise, and the cleverness of the clever I will set aside." 1 Corinthians 1:19

Day's Reading: 1 Corinthians 1-4

First Corinthians is the earliest written book of the New Testament, written within 25 years of Christ's accent. That said, it is actually the second letter of Paul to the Corinthians (the first has not been preserved), a people for whom Paul had great concern. Corinthians were known as an immoral people. In fact, the word for *adulterous* and *Corinthian* was often used interchangeably. As the hub of commerce between Italy and Asia, Corinth could have been considered the New York City of the Roman world. The Corinthians Paul wrote to were indeed Christians, but they had a lot of overcoming and growing to do as new Christians in a corrupt society. Just because they believed in Jesus did not mean they were able to let go of all their immoral habits right away. It was a process—just as it is with us today. But God is faithful, and just as He did not give up on the Christians in Corinth, He will not give up on us.

Reflection:

- Can you think of someone who is a Christian but still living what appears to be the immoral life? How could you encourage them in the Lord as Paul did the Corinthians?
- Is there is an area of your life in which you defile the temple of God? If so, give it over to Him and pray for conviction and the power to make a change.

Prayer Guide:

- Ask for the power and conviction to turn from sin.
- Request courage to encourage others in the Lord.
- Ask for an understanding of God's Word that leads to personal application.
- Pray for your friends' prayer requests/needs.
- Request wisdom regarding your children's friendships and influences.
- Submit your day's activities to Him.

Memory Verse Goals:

- Repeat the verse of the week phrase by phrase five times.

Day 60

Or do you not know that your body is a temple of the Holy Spirit who is in you, whom you have from God, and that you are not your own? For you have been bought with a price: therefore glorify God in your body. 1 Corinthians 6:19-20

Day's Reading: 1 Corinthians 5-8

Glorify: to honor, to worship, to praise, to give all the glory, to give all the recognition, to exalt above all others. To glorify. Your body and your spirit includes your mind, your thoughts, your emotions, your stomach, your muscles, your bones—everything about you. Whatever you think, say, wear, eat, or do, let it glorify God. Is that not powerful? Everything you do, everything you are, everything you think, should bring God glory. I don't know about you, but that sounds like a life purpose if I've ever heard one. Now comes the praying and giving of our lives over to God so that step-by-step every day we glorify God a little more than the day before. Think of it as training for eternity because when we reach our final destination, that is all we will be doing—glorifying God with all our hearts, souls, and minds. Glory to God!

Reflection:

- Think through your day. How do you and/or can you glorify God even in the little things?
- What do you need to give over to God so that your body can more fully glorify Him?

Prayer Guide:

- Praise God for who He is and His grace upon you.

- Ask for perseverance and wisdom in all you do so as to give Him praise.
- Share with Him your heart — that you desire it to be filled with greater love and compassion for your children, your spouse, and those around you.
- Surrender your spouse's heart--that it would be filled with greater love and compassion for you and your children.
- Relinquish your children's hearts — that they would be filled with greater love and compassion for their siblings and others.
- Submit your day's activities to Him.

Memory Verse Goals:

- Say the verse of the week aloud twenty times in a row.

Day 61

*Do you not know that those who run in a race all run,
but only one receives the prize? Run in such a way that you
may win. 1 Corinthians 9:24*

Day's Reading: 1 Corinthians 9-12

Sometimes I feel like I should have more urgency in spreading the Good News. I mean those who run in a race run with urgency because they know the time is short and others are doing the same. They also run because they want the prize or medal at the end. For us as Christians, the medal isn't salvation; that's a gift (see Romans 4:1-8). For us, the prize is the crown of righteousness (2 Timothy 4:8, Matthew 5:10-12) awarded for endurance. For what? Endurance — sticking it out to the end — not speed.

Today my hubby is running in a half marathon — what many refer to as a long-distance race not a speed run. As I gave him a few last words of encouragement, he commented, "I'm doing this just for fun."

I replied, "I know, but I still want you to do your best." And you know, I think that's really what God wants from us — for us to do our best. My husband trained hard, completing speed drills as well as long distance runs week after week in preparation for this day. He kept at it so that at the end he would obtain nothing more than a finisher's medal — a medal that says, "I did it. I kept on keeping on." That's what the crown of righteousness will be like — a finisher's medal. A medal that says we kept on living for Jesus and showing others His love even in the every day. Yes, we should have some urgency in sharing the Good News, but we also need to keep in mind that sharing the truth in love involves time and persistence and patience so that in the end it will be credited to us as righteousness.

Reflection:

- What are some ways you show others Jesus' love in the every day?
- Are you taking time to train every day too? If so, how?

Prayer Guide:

- Ask for endurance and urgency in the race of life.
- Pray for your and your spouse's safety, purity, and power to resist sexual and/or emotional temptation.
- Request help regarding your children's safety, wisdom, and purity.
- Pray for the safety and wisdom for the military and those you know in the military.
- Submit your day's activities to Him.

Memory Verse Goals:

- Review the verse of the week ten times in a row.
- Review Luke 21:33 (from week 6) and Acts 3:19 (from week 7) one time.
- Review James 3:17 (from week 8) two times.

Day 62

Be on the alert, stand firm in the faith, act like men, be strong. Let all that you do be done in love. 1 Corinthians 16:13-14

Day's Reading: 1 Corinthians 13-16

When you were little, do you remember ever playing dress up with your parents' clothing or trying to act like them? Or, have you seen this action in your children or other children around you? It is a natural reaction for children to want to grow up to be like their parents. It's natural and a great honor—an honor that comes with great responsibility because we want our children to imitate and do what is right.

Just as we are that example to our children, so Christ is that example for us. As Christians we should want to imitate Christ and His actions. In 1 Corinthians 16:13, it says to "be strong." These words could have also been translated "be the man" meaning we are to be Christ to those around us, standing strong in our faith (as He did), loving others (as He did), and anticipating the future (as He did). To be a true disciple or follower of Jesus is to be an imitator of Christ and act AS HE DID.

Reflection:

- How do you act like "the man" in your every day life?
- In what ways could you love another and/or be strong in the faith today as Jesus did while on earth?

Prayer Guide:

- Express your need for bravery in the faith.
- Request a love for others like Jesus' love.

- Ask for opportunities and confidence to show your spouse respect, grace, and kindness every day.
- Intercede for your children—that they would develop a heart of compassion, service, and prayer.
- Plead with God on behalf of the poor, hungry, and persecuted.
- Dedicate to God personally known city, state, national, and international mission efforts.
- Submit your day's activities to Him.

Memory Verse Goals:

- Review the verse of the week three times in a row.
- Review Acts 3:19 (from week 7) and James 3:17 (from week 8) one time.

Day 63

For God, who said, "Light shall shine out of darkness," is the
One who has shone in our hearts to give the Light of the
knowledge of the glory of God in the face of Christ.
2 Corinthians 4:6

Day's Reading: 2 Corinthians 1-4

"Then God said, 'Let there be light'; and there was light.
God saw that the light was good; and God separated the light
from the darkness" (Genesis 1:3-4). Do you remember those
verses from the story of Creation? Just as God created the
light in the darkness in this external world, He is also the one
responsible for creating the light from within the darkness of
our souls.

"The god of this world" (2 Corinthians 4:4), Satan, wants
to blind us from the light or knowledge of Jesus. However,
once we believe, Jesus removes the blinders so that we see the
light or the truth. As the old country song by Hank Williams
says, "Praise the Lord—I saw the light."

Reflection:

- Have you asked God to remove Satan's blinders in
  your heart? If not, do it today. It will make all the
  difference in the world.
- What is one indicator in your life that reveals that
  your heart bursts with the light of Christ? Can others
  see it too?

Prayer Guide:

- Praise God for personal spiritual victories found in
  your life and those around you.

- Ask for the "Light of the knowledge of the glory of God in the face of Christ" (2 Corinthians 4:6).
- Request power in the midst of current trials.
- Petition for your family's self-confidence and self-motivation to do and be what God desires
- Pray for your church and the leadership therein.
- Submit your day's activities to Him.

Memory Verse Goals:

- Review the verse of the week one time.
- Review Luke 2:52 (from week 1), John 12:26 (from week 5), Acts 3:19 (from week 7) and James 3:17 (from week 8) one time.

Week 10

For I am convinced that neither death, nor life, nor angels, nor principalities, nor things present, nor things to come, nor powers, nor height, nor depth, nor any other created thing, will be able to separate us from the love of God, which is in Christ Jesus our Lord.   Romans 8:38-39

Day 64

But just as you abound in everything, in faith and utterance and knowledge and in all earnestness and in the love we inspired in you, see that you abound in this gracious work also. 2 Corinthians 8:7

Day's Reading: 2 Corinthians 5-9

On occasion I hear other Christians mention how they don't set goals for their life because they "just leave it all in God's hands." While that sounds like a good motto, that is not exactly what the Lord meant about giving things over to Him. We are to "give" the stress and worries of life to God, not the striving or planning. That said, let me be clear — even in planning, we must know that all is contingent on God's will and that He may in fact change our plans because they don't line up with His goals. However, as Proverbs 16:9 and this passage in 2 Corinthians 8:10-12 declare, it is to our advantage to set goals and then strive to accomplish them — Lord willing. And what better outline for setting goals than 2 Corinthians 8:7 in which Paul outlines goals for growing in the faith, in speech, in knowledge, in diligence, in love, and in grace.

Reflection:

- What goals could you set for the next week, month, or year to motivate you to grow as suggested in 2 Corinthians 8:7?
- How can the setting and accomplishing of goals further the kingdom of God?

Prayer Guide:

- Ask for guidance and motivation in goal setting.

- Share with Him your longing for a heart filled with worship.
- Request His leadership regarding your family, your family's activities, and your family's goals.
- Ask for discipline to accomplish your personal goals, Lord willing.
- Submit your day's activities to Him.

Memory Verse Goals:

- Read the verse of the week five times.
- Post the verse of the week in a prominent location.

Day 65

But he who boasts is to boast in the Lord. 2 Corinthians 10:17

Day's Reading: 2 Corinthians 10-13

I once heard it said that nothing disqualifies us more from spiritual usefulness than pride. Only God knows how true that statement really is, but the person who once spoke it made a good point—when we are focused on ourselves and our accomplishments, we are not focusing on Christ, His accomplishments, and how we can draw others to Him. Today's key verse, 2 Corinthians 10:17, is actually a partial quote of Jeremiah 9:23-24 which says:

> *Thus says the LORD, "Let not a wise man boast of his wisdom, and let not the mighty man boast of his might, let not a rich man boast of his riches; but let him who boasts boast of this, that he understands and knows Me, that I am the LORD who exercises loving kindness, justice and righteousness on earth; for I delight in these things," declares the LORD.*

In this whole passage Paul is boasting about his weaknesses (2 Corinthians 12:5), but he's doing so to make a point—that God's grace is sufficient and His strength is perfect (2 Corinthians 12:9). Yes, you may have much to boast about, and you may have accomplished a lot or have been through a lot, but in the end, it's really not so much about YOU as it is about HIM. So next time you get ready to boast about something in your life, first think—how does this show God's grace and love? If you can't think of a reason, then maybe it would be better if you said nothing at all.

Reflection:

- What are some current events/situations in which you could boast about Christ's love, grace, strength, and/or sufficiency?
- Is there an area you need to give over to Jesus because pride is preventing you from being spiritually useful?

Prayer Guide:

- Praise God for His greatness.
- Ask for humility of heart and mind.
- Pray for a development of an eternal perspective in you and your family members.
- Request health and salvation for your family members.
- Ask for wisdom in teaching your children about loyalty and responsibility.
- Submit your day's activities to Him.

Memory Verse Goals:

- Look up any unfamiliar words or meanings found in the verse of the week.
- Pray and meditate on the verse of the week.

Day 66

...even the righteousness of God through faith in Jesus Christ for all those who believe; for there is no distinction; for all have sinned and fall short of the glory of God, being justified as a gift by His grace through the redemption which is in Christ Jesus. Romans 3:22-24

Day's Reading: Acts 20:1-3, Romans 1-3

It was 57 A.D. in Rome. Much like a modern day New York City, Rome was the hub of commerce and a major port city. The ancient world viewed Rome as the leader of modern society much like many view Hollywood or New York City in North America today. Many scholars today believe that the Christians in Rome were most likely established by some excited new believers who had come from Jerusalem. Although growing quietly and excitedly for the Lord, they had very little formal training in the truth from scripture and/or the apostles. Thus, the book of Romans was Paul's attempt to provide them a solid well-instructed foundation from which to grow. Written to a rather diverse group of Christians, Paul's overarching statement throughout is that God justifies and ultimately glorifies those who come to Him through faith by grace.

Reflection:

- Sometimes we forget that telling others about the Good News doesn't have to be by word of mouth. The "telling" of the Good News could be in the form of a letter, an email, or even a tweet. Is there someone you could share the Gospel with today by using the written word much like Paul did to the Roman Christians?

- Many have memorized Romans 3:23 but few realize the context in which the verse is spoken. How does the addition of Romans 3:24 change and/or solidify your understanding of Romans 3:23?

Prayer Guide:

- Thank God for the justification and grace of Jesus.
- Pray for an opportunity to share the gospel through the written word.
- Ask for an understanding of God's Word that leads to personal application.
- Request spiritual, mental, and emotional health for you and your family members.
- Pray for your neighbors' prayer requests/needs.
- Submit your day's activities to Him.

Memory Verse Goals:

- Repeat the verse of the week phrase by phrase five times.

Day 67

*But God demonstrates His own love toward us, in that while
we were yet sinners, Christ died for us. Romans 5:8*

Day's Reading: Romans 4-7

Romans 5:8 is one of the most quoted passages of
scripture thanks to the Roman Road and other tracts geared
towards guiding others to salvation. Its power is nearly
unprecedented as it sums up the entire gospel in a single
sentence. Yet, have you ever noticed that "demonstrates" is
in the present tense and active voice, not past tense? God's
love is ever active. It's something that is happening now and
forever. In contrast Paul uses past tense when referring to
Jesus' death—He "died" for us. His death and resurrection
was all that was needed to assure our salvation, but His love
for us didn't stop there. It continues every day. Why?
Because God is God. God loves you day in and day out
because of who He is—God is love (1 John 4:8). God's love is
not a result of our character, or our way of living, or what we
do. God's love is a result of God's character, and that is why
He loves us…no…matter…what.

Reflection:

- Have you ever been "saved from wrath" (Romans 5:9)
  through Christ's love? If so, how have you seen His
  love demonstrated again and again?
- With whom can you share some of the ways Christ
  has demonstrated His love to you?

Prayer Guide:

- Thank God for His indescribable gift.
- Ask for courage to share the Good News of Christ's
  love with others.

- Request wisdom regarding your family's finances and discipline to use the money God's given you for His glory.
- Pray for the moral integrity of the next generation.
- Surrender to God your children's future mates.
- Submit your day's activities to Him.

Memory Verse Goals:

- Say the verse of the week aloud twenty times in a row.

Day 68

And we know that God causes all things to work together for good to those who love God, to those who are called according to His purpose. Romans 8:28

Day's Reading: Romans 8-10

Life has a way of throwing curve balls. Sometimes even a lot of curve balls. Some are stressful. Others are depressing. A few are even painful. Yet God says, "ALL things work together for good to those who love God" (personal emphasis added). Do you know the difference between a Christian and a non-Christian? Hope—hope in the future, hope in an eternal plan, hope in God. Non-Christians don't have that hope. Oh, they may think they have that life-giving hope for a short time, but it soon fades. Knowing Jesus is different—our hope allows God to use everything—EVERYTHING—even the yuckiest of life's experiences to remind us once again of our desperate need of Him and develop a stronger love for Him in our hearts. And what a hope He gives because, unlike a wish, we know it will indeed happen. Glory to God! I can't wait!

Reflection:

- What situation(s) in your life right now seem hopeless? How do you think God might be able to turn the situation into a hopeful one?
- What situations in your past have you seen the hope of Jesus shine through as time progressed?

Prayer Guide:

- Thank God for the hope of Jesus.

- Pray for patience and perseverance through current circumstances in hope of the future.
- Request physical strength and health for you, your spouse, and your children.
- Surrender to God your city, state, and national governments and the current issues therein.
- Pray for world leaders, events, and concerns.
- Submit your day's activities to Him.

Memory Verse Goals:

- Review the verse of the week ten times in a row.
- Review Acts 3:19 (from week 7) and James 3:17 (from week 8) one time
- Review 1 Corinthians 10:13 (from week 9) two times

Day 69

*Therefore I urge you, brethren, by the mercies of God,
to present your bodies a living and holy sacrifice, acceptable to
God, which is your spiritual service of worship. And do not be
conformed to this world, but be transformed by the renewing
of your mind, so that you may prove what the will of God is,
that which is good and acceptable and perfect. Romans 12:1-2*

Day's Reading: Romans 11-13

The stage is set. The scene is beautiful. You are sitting on
a pew next to complete strangers as the moment arrives.
Everyone rises to watch in eager expectation as the bride,
dressed in a glorious white dress, slowly walks down the
center aisle. The ritual lasts for only a moment, but it's
completion will not soon be forgotten.

Worship is like a wedding. When you take the time to
show up, you are doing so to give Him honor, to give Him
respect, to give Him your services. In today's passage, the
original Greek for "spiritual service" refers to a priest's
duties, which is why some translate it as "spiritual service of
worship" or "spiritual act of worship." To serve God is to
worship Him.

Reflection:

- How could you serve God today as an act of worship?
- What things "of this world" do you need to let go in
  order to better follow God's will?

Prayer Guide:

- Praise God for who He is to you.

- Request forgiveness for worldly actions and strength to make a change.
- Ask for the Lord's blessing/enablement in your family's life roles.
- Pray for your family's energy, enthusiasm, and success in career settings.
- Surrender to God your children's education and those involved in their education.
- Submit your day's activities to Him.

Memory Verse Goals:

- Review the verse of the week three times in a row.
- Review James 3:17 (from week 8) and 1 Corinthians 10:13 (from week 9) one time.

Day 70

...for if we live, we live for the Lord, or if we die, we die for the Lord; therefore whether we live or die, we are the Lord's.
Romans 14:8

Day's Reading: Romans 14-16

Where do your kids go to school? Public? Private? Charter? Homeschool? What kind of food do you eat? Organic? Local? Commercial? Fast? Do you observe a Sabbath? If so, when? Saturday? Sunday? Some other weekday? A little every day? Just as in the time of the book of Romans, there are so many topics on which we could judge and do judge others. But to judge is not our job; it's God's. Our concern should be to make sure whatever WE are doing WE do it for the Lord. And we also need to remember that another Christian may indeed be doing all they do for the Lord even though their life may look completely different from our own. I love this summarizing thought in Romans 14:13:

> *Therefore let us not judge one another anymore, but rather determine this — not to put an obstacle or a stumbling block in a brother's way.*

Reflection:

- Is there an area in your life that is not glorifying God, or that could be viewed by a young Christian as a stumbling block in his/her Christian walk? What could you do to change that area of your life to better glorify God?
- Is there an area of your life that sometimes gives you a "holier-than-thou" attitude towards others? That is pride. Pray for humility of heart and compassion (understanding for others) in its place.

Prayer Guide:

- Petition for a respect and compassion for other Christians who are also working out their salvation.
- Request humility of heart and wisdom for upcoming decisions.
- Ask for boldness and sensitivity to reach the lost and needy around you.
- Dedicate your church's ministries to Him.
- Pray for sensitivity to serve where needed in your community and/or church.
- Submit your day's activities to Him.

Memory Verse Goals:

- Review the verse of the week one time.
- Review Matthew 5:16 (from week 2), Luke 21:33 (from week 6), James 3:17 (from week 8) and 1 Corinthians 10:13 (from week 9) one time.

Week 11

Whatever you do, do your work heartily, as for the Lord rather than for men, knowing that from the Lord you will receive the reward of the inheritance. It is the Lord Christ whom you serve. Colossians 3:23-24

Day 71

"In everything I showed you that by working hard in this manner you must help the weak and remember the words of the Lord Jesus, that He Himself said, 'It is more blessed to give than to receive.'" Acts 20:35

Day's Reading: Acts 20:4-23:35

The Christmas season, the season of giving, is quickly approaching as I write these words. In fact, just yesterday my daughter and I had a conversation about how "it is more blessed to give than to receive" and "'tis the season for giving not getting." She didn't seem to agree. In her four year old mind, Christmas is all about the presents and the getting, not the giving. And, if we were really doing a heart check on ourselves, I imagine inwardly many of us think that selfish way as well. "Maybe this Christmas I'll finally get a bonus so I can buy..." or "Maybe this Christmas my spouse will finally get me...." Yes, even we often lose the meaning of Jesus' words in the busy-ness of the Christmas hustle and bustle.

That said, are you ready for a shocker? These words of Jesus were never recorded in the gospels. That's right. Paul is the only one who ever made reference to the phrase, "it is more blessed to give than to receive." How shocking, yet how appropriate as Paul gave up nearly all to follow Christ. He, of all people, knew that it was indeed "more blessed to give than to receive."

Reflection:

- Who could you give something to this week?
- What could you do or give with your children to demonstrate to them the meaning behind Jesus' words about giving?

Prayer Guide:

- Ask for forgiveness for a selfish heart.
- Pray for a giving heart.
- Express your desire for personal spiritual growth, sensitivity to sin, and discipline to maintain a daily quiet time.
- Intercede for your spouse's spiritual growth, sensitivity to sin, and spiritual leadership.
- Pray for your children's spiritual growth and sensitivity to sin.
- Submit your day's activities to Him.

Memory Verse Goals:

- Read the verse of the week five times.
- Post the verse of the week in a prominent location.

Day 72

So, having obtained help from God, I stand to this day testifying both to small and great, stating nothing but what the Prophets and Moses said was going to take place; that the Christ was to suffer, and that by reason of His resurrection from the dead He would be the first to proclaim light both to the Jewish people and to the Gentiles."
Acts 26:22-23

Day's Reading: Acts 24-26

If ever there were a testimony that had more impact on the world than any other, it would have to be Paul's. And yet, what amazes me more than his testimony is how and when he shares it with others — kings, religious leaders, and governors. He does not shirk from sharing the good news of Jesus even though he knows his sharing will often result in persecution, imprisonment, and eventually death. How many times have I resisted sharing the gospel for the sake of pride or possible pain? I don't know about you, but I have never been beaten or imprisoned for sharing the gospel. Too often my mind sends thoughts like "it's their own decision" or "what will they think of me?" or "how will this change our relationship?" instead of "what can I share with this person that God has done in my life?" Oh Father, forgive us for being so selfish and proud. Humble us and give us the boldness we need to share with others about you.

Reflection:

- What is your testimony? How has Jesus transformed your life? Consider writing it down as you think it through.
- With whom could you share your testimony this week?

Prayer Guide:

- Ask for boldness to share the Gospel with others.
- Pray for softened hearts willing to be changed by the gospel.
- Request wisdom for you, your spouse, and your children regarding your time, talents, spiritual gifts, and finances.
- Pray for your family's prayer requests/needs.
- Submit your day's activities to Him.

Memory Verse Goals:

- Look up any unfamiliar words or meanings found in the verse of the week.
- Pray and meditate on the verse of the week.

Day 73

And he stayed two full years in his own rented quarters and was welcoming all who came to him, preaching the kingdom of God and teaching concerning the Lord Jesus Christ with all openness, unhindered. Acts 28:30-31

Day's Reading: Acts 27-28

I once knew a lady who in her old age had a rather hard time getting around, especially during her later years. She loved coming to church, but as her mobility continued to decrease she found it difficult to maneuver the crowds and would often venture out only on special occasions. Yet there were three things that separated this women from many other aging women I know: her genuine smile, her heart for seeing little ones come to Jesus, and her perseverance to reach the next generation no matter what. How many 85-year old women do you know willing to buy a computer, learn how to use Facebook and Twitter, and then use them to encourage others in the Lord daily? Well, that is exactly what my dear friend did every day for the remainder of her life. Even when she could no longer teach a Sunday school class or serve cookies in the Vacation Bible School snack line or sit on the front pew with the orphaned and widowed, from home she still served the Lord whole-heartedly much like Paul…to all who came to her. Oh how different this world might be if more of us realized that serving God doesn't stop at the door; it's forever and in every circumstance and for all who will hear. May more of us grow to be like my friend whose impact I will never forget.

Reflection:

- How can you reach out to others for Jesus today?

- Whom do you know in your life who has set a Paul-like example for you, reaching to all who will hear? How can you emulate them?

Prayer Guide:

- Ask for boldness to share the Gospel with others.
- Pray for wisdom in where and how to share the Good News with others.
- Ask for an understanding of God's Word that leads to personal application.
- Pray for your friends' prayer requests/needs.
- Request wisdom regarding your children's friendships and influences.
- Submit your day's activities to Him.

Memory Verse Goals:

- Repeat the verse of the week phrase by phrase five times.

Day 74

Whatever you do in word or deed, do all in the name of the Lord Jesus, giving thanks through Him to God the Father.
Colossians 3:17

Day's Reading: Colossians 1-4, Philemon

I love Colossians and Paul's blunt explanations of what it means to be a Christian. Sometimes we get so bogged down with legalities that we forget the truth of what it means to live for Jesus. It's not about when you enjoy a Sabbath, what you eat or how you worship; it's how you live. That reminds me of a song by Point of Grace in which they sing, "Because it's not who you knew and it's not what you did. It's how you live." Do you live for Jesus or do you live for something or someone else? What gets you most excited about your day? Whom do you serve? Colossians 3:17 sums it up great — "Whatever you do...do it for Jesus" because in the end, that's all that will really matter.

Reflection:

- In what area(s) of your life do you need to adjust your actions or thoughts to better give God the glory?
- What legalistic regulations do you need to let go in your life and let God take over?

Prayer Guide:

- Pray for a speech filled with grace and seasoned with salt (Colossians 4:6).
- Ask for wisdom and freedom from the legalism of Christianity.

- Share with Him your heart — that you desire it to be filled with greater love and compassion for your children, your spouse, and those around you.
- Surrender your spouse's heart — that it would be filled with greater love and compassion for you and your children.
- Relinquish your children's hearts — that they would be filled with greater love and compassion for their siblings and others.
- Submit your day's activities to Him.

Memory Verse Goals:

- Say the verse of the week aloud twenty times in a row.

Day 75

For by grace you have been saved through faith; and that not of yourselves, it is the gift of God; not as a result of works, so that no one may boast. Ephesians 2:8-9

Day's Reading: Ephesians 1-6

Which comes first—faith or grace? This issue has always been sticky throughout the history of Christianity, but according to this verse the answer is grace. It is the grace of God that saves us, not our faith. However, faith is the foundation of that grace. I will never forget the first time I was presented with this realization and it clicked. I was on a road trip with a friend reading *Future Grace* by John Piper when I looked up and asked my friend the exact same question I asked at the beginning of this paragraph. A great discussion followed. See, if it's all about faith, it's all about you and what you can do to obtain salvation via the strength of your own faith. But, if it's all about grace, it's all about God and what He did on the cross to save you. Put the two together and the result is amazing salvation! Yes, we cannot do anything to earn salvation. It is a gift. God has already made the gift, wrapped it and prepared the party. All we need to do is show up and receive the gift with thankfulness and trust. What amazing grace is God's love for us!

Reflection:

- Is there an area of your Christian walk in which you have let pride take over grace? What do you need to give back to God to give Him the rightful place on the throne as the grace-giver?
- Is there an area of your life that you struggle submitting to God and/or others (Ephesians 5:21)? Pray for God to take control.

Prayer Guide:

- Thank God for His grace.
- Pray on the Armor of God (Ephesians 6:11-17).
- Pray for your and your spouse's safety, purity, and power to resist sexual and/or emotional temptation.
- Request help regarding your children's safety, wisdom, and purity.
- Pray for the safety and wisdom for the military and those you know in the military.
- Submit your day's activities to Him.

Memory Verse Goals:

- Review the verse of the week ten times in a row.
- Review James 3:17 (from week 8) and 1 Corinthians 10:13 (from week 9) one time.
- Review Romans 8:38-39 (from week 10) two times.

Day 76

Rejoice in the Lord always; again I will say, rejoice!
Philippians 4:4

Day's Reading: Philippians 1-4

The predominant theme of Philippians is rejoicing in the Lord. In fact, sixteen times joy and/or rejoice are mentioned in this short book. And oddly enough, Paul wrote this book while in prison. Yes, even then Paul was a cheerleader for the Lord and the Philippians, making it a great book to read on a day you are feeling discouraged, or any day. Whatever you are facing (death, sickness, discouragement, frustration), rejoice because God is with you and God is for you! Rejoice and again I say, rejoice!

Reflection:

- There are several well-known verses in Philippians. Today take a look at a few in light of Philippians 4:4. How does Philippians 2:1-4, 14-15, 3:8, and 4:6-8 read in light of Paul's encouraging demeanor while imprisoned?
- In what areas of your life do you need to turn your thoughts and expectations from gloom and doom to rejoicing?

Prayer Guide:

- Rejoice! Praise God for Who He is and all He's done.
- Pray Philippians 1:9-11 for yourself, your husband, and your children.
- Ask for opportunities and confidence to show your spouse respect, grace, and kindness every day.

- Intercede for your children—that they would develop a heart of compassion, service, and prayer.
- Plead with God on behalf of the poor, hungry, and persecuted.
- Dedicate to God personally known city, state, national, and international mission efforts.
- Submit your day's activities to Him.

Memory Verse Goals:

- Review the verse of the week three times in a row.
- Review 1 Corinthians 10:13 (from week 9) and Romans 8:38-39 (from week 10) one time.

Day 77

First of all, then, I urge that entreaties and prayers,
petitions and thanksgivings, be made on behalf of all men, for
kings and all who are in authority, so that we may lead a
tranquil and quiet life in all godliness and dignity.
1 Timothy 2:1-2

Day's Reading: 1 Timothy 1-6

If there is one area in my spiritual life that I really need to spend more time on, it's prayer, and what better outline for prayer than the one given here in 1 Timothy. Growing up, I used to hear the following acronym as a prayer guide:

Adoration

Confession

Thanksgiving

Supplication

Here in 1 Timothy, Paul provides a similar outline. "Entreaties" emphasize personal needs or supplication regarding one's self. "Prayers" refer to the general attitudes of adoration or worship as directed towards God. "Petitions" suggest the offering of requests for others or supplication regarding others. And "thanksgiving" is the expression of recognition and gratitude for all that God has done. I also find it particularly interesting, although very appropriate, that Paul adds a reference to not only pray for ALL men (Christian and non-Christian alike), but also to pray for governmental leadership. I once heard it said that if we are serious about changing our nation for good, then we've got to get serious about prayer. So with that said, let's get our prayer on and start changing the world for God. The spiritual battle is on.

Reflection:

- When do you set aside time to pray?
- Although Paul didn't mention it in 1 Timothy 2:1-2, he later mentions confession in the phrase "lifting up holy hands" in 1 Timothy 2:8 which means to pray with a morally and spiritually clean heart. And what better way to do that than by beginning with the cleaning of your heart through confession to the Lord. What do you need to confess to God to begin your prayer time today?

Prayer Guide:

- Use the outline expressed in 1 Timothy 2:1-2 to guide your prayers today.
- Praise God for personal spiritual victories found in your life and those around you.
- Pray for wisdom for your governmental leadership.
- Relinquish to God each immediate family member's self-confidence and self-motivation to do and be what He wants them to be.
- Pray for your church and the leadership therein.
- Submit your day's activities to Him.

Memory Verse Goals:

- Review the verse of the week one time.
- Review Mark 8:34 (from week 3), Acts 3:19 (from week 7), 1 Corinthians 10:13 (from week 9), and Romans 8:38-39 (from week 10) one time.

Week 12

Therefore humble yourselves under the mighty hand of God, that He may exalt you at the proper time, casting all your anxiety on Him, because He cares for you.   1 Peter 5:6-7

Day 78

Remind them to be subject to rulers, to authorities, to be obedient, to be ready for every good deed, to malign no one, to be peaceable, gentle, showing every consideration for all men.
Titus 3:1-2

Day's Reading: Titus 1-3

As Titus 1:12-13 explains, Cretans were known as disrespectful liars and the world's worst citizens. Thus Paul and Titus both advised new Cretan Christians to be just the opposite so that others would see Jesus in them. One of the most quoted verses for women, Titus 2:3-5, also supports this claim—whatever we do, we should do it out of love, respect, and purity of heart "so that the word of God will not be dishonored." Just as in the pagan society of Crete where the Cretan Christians showed Jesus to others by their actions, so, too, we should show Jesus to our neighbors in all we do.

Reflection:

- What kind of impression do you think your neighbors currently have of you based upon your current actions? Is it accurate? Is it reflective of God or something else?
- Probably one of the most challenging parts of Titus 3:1-2, at least for me, is to "to malign no one" or speak ill of no one or any situation. Consider challenging yourself to refrain from negative talk about anyone this week so as to see what difference it makes in your relationship with God and others.

Prayer Guide:

- Ask for an obedient and pure heart.

- Express your desire to honor God in your actions.
- Share with Him your longing for a heart filled with worship.
- Request His leadership regarding your family, your family's activities, and your family's goals.
- Ask for discipline to accomplish your personal goals, Lord willing.
- Submit your day's activities to Him.

Memory Verse Goals:

- Read the verse of the week five times.
- Post the verse of the week in a prominent location.

Day 79

To sum up, all of you be harmonious,
sympathetic, brotherly, kindhearted, and humble in spirit; not
returning evil for evil or insult for insult, but giving
a blessing instead; for you were called for the very purpose
that you might inherit a blessing. 1 Peter 3:8-9

Day's Reading: 1 Peter 1-5

At one time I used to think that 1 Peter 3:8-9 would be the perfect wedding verse. In a way, I suppose I still do because marriage is much like life — you have to learn to give and give and give some more without expecting much in return. In these verses Peter emphasizes the contrast between our human tendency to "get even" when offended with the importance of our being kind like Jesus because how we behave defines a big part of who we are. Are we kind and compassionate like Jesus? Or, are we pushy, rude, and selfish like Satan? What it really boils down to is — have we allowed the world to define who we are or Jesus? Our actions tell all so let's make them good ones.

Reflection:

- Are you being selfish or proud in a specific situation with your spouse, a friend, or a neighbor? How would Jesus want you to respond differently?
- Life is hard and sometimes almost unbearable. What struggles do you need to give to God because "He cares for you" (1 Peter 5:7)?

Prayer Guide:

- Pray for courage and humility to be kind and compassionate even when it's hard.

- Ask for strength to walk like Jesus even in the midst of the struggles of life.
- Pray for a development of an eternal perspective in you and your family members.
- Request health and salvation for your family members.
- Ask for wisdom in teaching your children about loyalty and responsibility.
- Submit your day's activities to Him.

Memory Verse Goals:

- Look up any unfamiliar words or meanings found in the verse of the week.
- Pray and meditate on the verse of the week.

Day 80

For the word of God is living and active and sharper than any two-edged sword, and piercing as far as the division of soul and spirit, of both joints and marrow, and able to judge the thoughts and intentions of the heart. Hebrews 4:12

Day's Reading: Hebrews 1-5

Over the last few days I have encountered more trials than I've liked, making me one stressed mama. Thus, when a dear friend called to encourage me, I spilled all. "How can we pray for you, Kathy?" was the beginning. I then asked for discernment and peace over the many situations that seemed to have risen all at the same time. She then proceeded to pray over me right then and there on the phone. Upon hanging up, she looked up some relevant scriptures and emailed them to me. It was only when I read the encouraging words of scripture in her email that my heart finally broke. The tears began to fall, and a peace finally started to take over. By the end of the day, those many stressing situations were starting to appear manageable again. Yes, God's word is definitely "sharper than any two-edged sword" (Hebrews 4:12).

Sometimes we try to manage life on our own, share our own eloquent words with those in pain, or turn to others or things for comfort instead of relying on God's Word. Yet, as this passage emphasizes, never underestimate the power of the Word. It can changes lives. It can change you.

Reflection:

- Do you ever find yourself overwhelmed by a situation? Consider using a sheet of paper, index card, or a notebook to write down some of your favorite Bible verses that you can then refer to in those times you need encouragement most.

- Just like a sport or a new skill must be practiced over and over for us to become good at it, so too we must exercise or "practice" over and over those spiritual disciplines so as to instill positive habits and discern truth (Hebrews 5:14). What spiritual habits do you need to focus on exercising more so that you are ready when life's struggles come your way?

Prayer Guide:

- Pray for discernment and peace in the midst life's struggles.
- Ask for an understanding of God's Word that leads to personal application.
- Request spiritual, mental, and emotional health for you and your family members.
- Pray for your neighbors' prayer requests/needs.
- Submit your day's activities to Him.

Memory Verse Goals:

- Repeat the verse of the week phrase by phrase five times.

Day 81

But when Christ appeared as a high priest of the good
things to come, He entered through the greater and more
perfect tabernacle, not made with hands, that is to say, not of
this creation. Hebrews 9:11

Day's Reading: Hebrews 6-9

Hebrews is the one book of the New Testament whose
authorship is unknown. However, it won its place in the
New Testament on its merit and its answers to several
important questions concerning salvation in Christ versus the
Old Testament law. What laws should Christians still obey?
What laws did Christ's salvation overcome? Christianity was
at first considered a Jewish sect, so it was hard for them to
distinguish where they were to draw the line. For many, the
book of Hebrews answered that question. Christ is the
Ultimate High Priest. Meaning—there is not a need for
another. Through Jesus' sacrifice, we have direct access to
God, the forgiveness of sins, and an everlasting inheritance.
Why do we not need to offer animal sacrifices anymore?
Because Jesus was the ultimate sacrifice for us.

Reflection:

- Imagine what it would be like to have been a Jewish
  Christian in approximately 50 A.D. What theological
  struggles might you have had to work through? How
  are they similar and/or different from the struggles
  you currently have to maneuver through to work out
  your salvation (Philippians 2:12)?
- How does the image of Christ as the Ultimate High
  Priest impact the way you view Jesus or relate to Him?

Prayer Guide:

- Thank God for Christ's ultimate sacrifice on the cross.
- Request wisdom regarding your family's finances and discipline to use the money God's given you for His glory.
- Pray for the moral integrity of the next generation.
- Surrender to God your children's future mates.
- Submit your day's activities to Him.

Memory Verse Goals:

- Say the verse of the week aloud twenty times in a row.

Day 82

And let us consider how to stimulate one another to love and good deeds, not forsaking our own assembling together, as is the habit of some, but encouraging one another; and all the more as you see the day drawing near. Hebrews 10:24-25

Day's Reading: Hebrews 10-13

Christians are the worst at hurting other Christians. Believe me, I've had my fair share of painful circumstances within the church — hurtful words, false rumors, critical eyes. They all seem to stab the heart such that some never come back. A dear friend of mine once told me, "Jesus I believe. The church — not so much."

But that outlook of the church, resulting from hurts within, is not how the church is supposed to work. Jesus is love, so therefore, we are called to love. I think as Christians we sometimes get so caught up in the hurt-filled cycle because we think if someone is a Christian we should be able to expect more from them. What we forget is that other Christians are still sinners saved by grace just like you and me. We need each other. And Jesus needs us to need each other too so that He can use others to encourage us in Him and show the world that His love really does make a difference. So, do we really need to go to church this week? The answer is a resounding yes.

Reflection:

- Whom could you be an encouragement to at church this week?
- Is there someone whom you may have hurt in the church to whom you need to apologize and/or pray for?

Prayer Guide:

- Intercede on behalf of your church community.
- Request physical strength and health for you, your spouse, and your children.
- Surrender to God your city, state, and national governments and the current issues therein.
- Pray for world leaders, events, and concerns.
- Submit your day's activities to Him.

Memory Verse Goals:

- Review the verse of the week ten times in a row.
- Review 1 Corinthians 10:13 (from week 9) and Romans 8:38-39 (from week 10) one time.
- Review Colossians 3:23-24 (from week 11) two times.

Day 83

All Scripture is inspired by God and profitable for teaching, for reproof, for correction, for training in righteousness.
2 Timothy 3:16

Day's Reading: 2 Timothy 1-4

The spiritual discipline of studying the Bible is important for four reasons:

1. It contains a wealth of knowledge and is a great teaching tool.
2. Its purity can bring correction of sin.
3. Its truth can point us in the right direction.
4. It tells us what is right and wrong so that we know which path to follow.

Did you notice that only one of these reasons focuses on worldly wisdom? The rest all focus on the changing of a life. The study of scripture should change you. I know people who have a daily "quiet time" just so they can check it off their to-do list. (Shoot, I'm even guilty of this in my own life on occasion). However, the truth of the matter is, it's worthless unless we allow all four aspects of scripture to change us for His glory. Otherwise, we are just reading a number-one seller over and over again — something you could do with any good book. Instead, pray, be attentive, and focus on what God is trying to tell you through His word each day. It could change your life.

Reflection:

- What did you learn and/or how did God use today's passage to convict you of sin?
- What are you going to do today as a result of your contact with the truth?

Prayer Guide:

- Ask for the forgiveness of sin.
- Request life-altering inspiration from scripture.
- Ask for the Lord's blessing/enablement in your family's life roles.
- Pray for your family's energy, enthusiasm, and success in career settings.
- Surrender to God your children's education and those involved in their education.
- Submit your day's activities to Him.

Memory Verse Goals:

- Review the verse of the week three times in a row.
- Review Romans 8:38-39 (from week 10) and Colossians 3:23-24 (from week 11) one time.

Day 84

Now for this very reason also, applying all diligence, in your faith supply moral excellence, and in your moral excellence, knowledge. 2 Peter 1:5

Day's Reading: 2 Peter 1-3, Jude

Life is full of false teachers. Just look on TV and you can find more than one preacher or teacher who is most likely a "Christian" for the buck rather than a follower of Christ unto salvation. Peter wrote 2 Peter because he struggled with false teachers and prophets. He knew how hard it was to turn back to the truth once exposed to false teaching. It messes with your mind so that it's hard to distinguish right from wrong.

As explained by the guide in 2 Peter 1:5, we should expect and pursue growth as Christians so that we do not become sidetracked with false doctrine. Our Christian life begins with faith, which eventually develops into virtue as we choose to obey the promptings of the Holy Spirit in us. Virtue is expanded in us as we study His Word and put it into action. Self-control, or the mastering of one's emotions, also develops with time as does perseverance. And all of these develop into godliness or a devoted life for God and not for ourselves, which ultimately leads us to living out that love with all people because God is love.

Reflection:

- I recently finished reading *Assumptions That Affect Our Lives* by Christian Overman. This book tosses out the window several of our modern day "Christian" beliefs that have been permeated with cultural influences over time forming a vein of false doctrine. Have you ever read something in scripture and thought to yourself "that can't be right" due to something you assumed or were taught before? If so, what? How did you overcome that false thought?

- In what situation do you need to ask God for self-control, perseverance, godliness, or brotherly kindness today?

Prayer Guide:

- Request each character trait in 2 Peter 1:5 for your own life.
- Pray for discernment to distinguish the truth from the lies.
- Ask for boldness and sensitivity to reach the lost and needy around you.
- Dedicate your church's ministries to Him.
- Pray for sensitivity to serve where needed in your community and/or church.
- Submit your day's activities to Him.

Memory Verse Goals:

- Review the verse of the week one time.
- Review John 8:31-32 (from week 4), James 3:17 (from week 8), Romans 8:38-39 (from week 10), and Colossians 3:23-24 (from week 11) one time.

Week 13

Beloved, let us love one another, for love is from God;
and everyone who loves is born of God and knows God. The
one who does not love does not know God, for God is love.
1 John 4:7-8

Day 85

This is His commandment that we believe in the name of His Son Jesus Christ, and love one another, just as He commanded us. 1 John 3:23

Day's Reading: 1 John 1-5

From the sound of it, John, Jude, and Peter were facing similar battles — false teachers. Gnosticism, a blended religion based on Eastern mysticism and Greek dualism, was rampant during the time of Peter and John just as Christianity and New Age are combining their beliefs in 21st century America to create a false religion all its own. Gnosticism contained enough spiritual truths to deceive but not enough to save as only the truth of Jesus can do.

How will people know that our belief in Jesus is real? By our love. How will we know our faith is real? By our humility that comes from knowing we are sinners in need of a Savior and our trust that Jesus Christ is that Savior (1 John 1:8-10). Just remember, there are lots of idols and false teachings out there. We all worship something, so make sure WHO you worship is the real deal.

Reflection:

- Who can you show Jesus' love to today?
- Do your actions show that your faith is real?

Prayer Guide:

- Pray for discernment of the truth from the false.
- Petition for an increased love for others.
- Confess your sins and express thankfulness for His salvation.

- Express your desire for personal spiritual growth, sensitivity to sin, and discipline to maintain a daily quiet time.
- Intercede for your spouse's spiritual growth, sensitivity to sin, and spiritual leadership.
- Pray for your children's spiritual growth and sensitivity to sin.
- Submit your day's activities to Him.

Memory Verse Goals:

- Read the verse of the week five times.
- Post the verse of the week in a prominent location.

Day 86

Anyone who goes too far and does not abide in the teaching of Christ, does not have God; the one who abides in the teaching, he has both the Father and the Son. 2 John 1:9

Day's Reading: 2 John, 3 John

Docetism was another false religion Christians battled during John's time. Docetists believed that Jesus was only a spirit that appeared human but really wasn't. Meaning, he never really suffered for us, He just went through the act. The most confusing thing about this belief was that docetists still claimed to be Christians. Maybe this was why in the gospel of John he emphasized "And the Word became flesh and dwelt among us" (John 1:14). Knowing that Jesus came as a human and was both completely God and completely man separates believers from non-believers. This is a truth we would do well to guard against as we continue to battle false teachings today.

Reflection:

- Can you think of a person or group who claims to be a Christian but whose fruit seems to suggest otherwise? What red flags do you see in their life to cause you to think this way?
- Are there any red flags in your own life you need to address so as to be a positive testimony for Jesus and not a hindrance?

Prayer Guide:

- Ask for a purity of heart and mind.

- Request wisdom for you, your spouse, and your children regarding your time, talents, spiritual gifts, and finances.
- Pray for your family's prayer requests/needs.
- Submit your day's activities to Him.

Memory Verse Goals:

- Look up any unfamiliar words or meanings found in the verse of the week.
- Pray and meditate on the verse of the week.

Day 87

And every created thing which is in heaven and on the earth and under the earth and on the sea, and all things in them, I heard saying, "To Him who sits on the throne, and to the Lamb, be blessing and honor and glory and dominion forever and ever."

Revelation 5:13

Day's Reading: Revelation 1-5

I can hardly imagine what heaven is going to be like, but it's going to be glorious! Have you ever had such an overwhelming love for someone that you burst into tears of joy upon seeing them? Or, have you ever become so excited about an event that you couldn't help but shout for joy? I sometimes imagine heaven will be like those feelings — where we are so overcome with love, joy, and excitement for our Lord that we can't help but burst forth in praise forever and ever. Just thinking about it gets me so giddy with joy that I may forget to wait for heaven and start praising Him right now. Oh wait…that's what He wants us to do! So let's go get our praise on today. Our God is an awesome God deserving of all glory and praise and honor forever and ever! Amen!

Reflection:

- What characteristic of God have you personally found evident in your life and could praise Him for today?
- Are you excited or nervous about heaven? Why?

Prayer Guide:

- Praise God for Who God is.
- Request a stronger eternal perspective on life.

- Ask for an understanding of God's Word that leads to personal application.
- Pray for your friends' prayer requests/needs.
- Request wisdom regarding your children's friendships and influences.
- Submit your day's activities to Him.

Memory Verse Goals:

- Repeat the verse of the week phrase by phrase five times.

Day 88

And they cry out with a loud voice, saying, "Salvation to our God who sits on the throne, and to the Lamb."
Revelation 7:10

Day's Reading: Revelation 6-11

As I sat reading today's passage, my heart fluctuated between "Oh, God, help us" and "Oh, God, I hope I don't have to live to see this." But to stay there would have limited one of the main purposes of this book, which is to remind us that God is in control of all history and all future. His ultimate goal—the establishment of the promised Messianic Kingdom. Praise God! He is indeed the first and the last. Salvation comes through and by Him alone!

Reflection:

- What are your immediate thoughts when reading this passage? How do they line up with God's ultimate goal—the establishment of the promised Messianic Kingdom?
- How does this passage encourage and/or prod you on your Christian walk?

Prayer Guide:

- Request courage to be strong in the Lord in the midst of tribulation.
- Pray for an active patience to wait until He returns.
- Share with Him your heart—that you desire it to be filled with greater love and compassion for your children, your spouse, and those around you.

- Surrender your spouse's heart — that it would be filled with greater love and compassion for you and your children.
- Relinquish your children's hearts — that they would be filled with greater love and compassion for their siblings and others.
- Submit your day's activities to Him.

Memory Verse Goals:

- Say the verse of the week aloud twenty times in a row.

Day 89

"Behold, I am coming like a thief. Blessed is the one who stays awake and keeps his clothes, so that he will not walk about naked and men will not see his shame." Revelation 16:15

Day's Reading: Revelation 12-17

Did you ever have a pop quiz when you were in school? What was the purpose? To see what you were really learning and how much you were studying on your own, right? Jesus' second coming is kind of like that pop quiz. You don't know when it's going to happen, but you can study a little every day just in case. With that in mind, let's try paraphrasing this verse a bit:

"Pay attention! Keep growing in the knowledge and wisdom of the Lord and living it out because Jesus is going to come back soon. Don't let His return surprise or embarrass you because of reckless behavior or worldly passions. Guard yourself against sin and the cares of this world. Strive to live righteously as Jesus would have you live. How embarrassing would it be if Jesus were to show up and you have nothing to show Him, the One who saved you? Don't be like someone taking a pop quiz who never took the time to prepare for it. The score—a big fat zero. Oh the shame."

Reflection:

- Would you be excited or embarrassed if Jesus were to return today? Why?
- What will you do today in preparation for His return?

Prayer Guide:

- Ask for a perseverance to keep growing in the truth.

- Pray for your and your spouse's safety, purity, and power to resist sexual and/or emotional temptation.
- Request help regarding your children's safety, wisdom, and purity.
- Pray for the safety and wisdom for the military and those you know in the military.
- Submit your day's activities to Him.

Memory Verse Goals:

- Review the verse of the week ten times in a row.
- Review Romans 8:38-39 (from week 10) and Colossians 3:23-24 (from week 11) one time.
- Review 1 Peter 5:6-7 (from week 12) two times.

Day 90

Then He said to me, "It is done. I am the Alpha and the Omega, the beginning and the end. I will give to the one who thirsts from the spring of the water of life without cost. He who overcomes will inherit these things, and I will be his God and he will be My son. Revelation 21:6-7

Day's Reading: Revelation 18-22

A to Z. The first and the last. The one who always was and always will be. This is the God whom we serve. He is the source of all things and in Him and only Him will we be made complete. He is the one who knows the beginning and the end because He establishes the beginning and the end. Our God is the only true God and His Son is the Savior of the entire world. Praise be to the God and Father of our Lord Jesus Christ. Praise Him for His great love for us for in Him all things will be made new. In Him there will be no more crying or pain or hurt. Oh what a glorious day we have to look forward to as believers in Christ. What blessed hope we have in Him.

Reflection:

- What characteristics of God most stand out to you in today's passage? Why?
- Who or what are you most looking forward to seeing in heaven?

Prayer Guide:

- Intercede on behalf of the martyrs of the Lord around the world.
- Request wisdom regarding personal preparation for His second coming .

- Ask for opportunities and confidence to show your spouse respect, grace, and kindness every day.
- Intercede for your children—that they would develop a heart of compassion, service, and prayer.
- Plead with God on behalf of the poor, hungry, and persecuted.
- Dedicate to God personally known city, state, national, and international mission efforts.
- Submit your day's activities to Him.

Memory Verse Goals:

- Review the verse of the week three times in a row.
- Review Colossians 3:23-24 (from week 11) and 1 Peter 5:6-7 (from week 12) one time.

Weekly Memory Verses

Week 1:   *And Jesus kept increasing in wisdom and stature, and in favor with God and men. Luke 2:52*

Week 2:   *Let your light shine before men in such a way that they may see your good works, and glorify your Father who is in heaven. Matthew 5:16*

Week 3:   *And He summoned the crowd with His disciples, and said to them, "If anyone wishes to come after Me, he must deny himself, and take up his cross and follow Me." Mark 8:34b*

Week 4:   *So Jesus was saying to those Jews who had believed Him, "If you continue in My word, then you are truly disciples of Mine; and you will know the truth, and the truth will make you free." John 8:31-32*

Week 5:   *"If anyone serves Me, he must follow Me; and where I am, there My servant will be also; if anyone serves Me, the Father will honor him." John 12:26*

Week 6:   *"Heaven and earth will pass away, but My words will not pass away." Luke 21:33*

Week 7:   *"Therefore repent and return, so that your sins may be wiped away, in order that times of refreshing may come from the presence of the Lord." Acts 3:19*

Week 8:   *But the wisdom from above is first pure, then peaceable, gentle, reasonable, full of mercy and good fruits, unwavering, without hypocrisy. James 3:17*

Week 9: *No temptation has overtaken you but such as is common to man; and God is faithful, who will not allow you to be tempted beyond what you are able, but with the temptation will provide the way of escape also, so that you will be able to endure it. 1 Corinthians 10:13*

Week 10: *For I am convinced that neither death, nor life, nor angels, nor principalities, nor things present, nor things to come, nor powers, nor height, nor depth, nor any other created thing, will be able to separate us from the love of God, which is in Christ Jesus our Lord. Romans 8:38-39*

Week 11: *Whatever you do, do your work heartily, as for the Lord rather than for men, knowing that from the Lord you will receive the reward of the inheritance. It is the Lord Christ whom you serve. Colossians 3:23-24*

Week 12: *Therefore humble yourselves under the mighty hand of God, that He may exalt you at the proper time, casting all your anxiety on Him, because He cares for you. 1 Peter 5:6-7*

Week 13: *Beloved, let us love one another, for love is from God; and everyone who loves is born of God and knows God. The one who does not love does not know God, for God is love. 1 John 4:7-8*

Acknowledgments

My loving Redeemer and friend—Jesus. Thank you for loving me and being patient with me, warts and all, as I learn what it means to be more like You in the every day.

My husband, for his support of me through the hours dedicated to the writing of this book.

My two precious little girls who teach me more about love and forgiveness than any other.

Cheryl Devoe and Donna Orrell for their English teacher expertise and encouragement in the editing of this book.

Steven VanCauwenbergh, author of *The Savvy Landlord,* for his book writing expertise and wisdom.

Aleta Biddy for her encouragement and wisdom as the spiritual mentor she has become.

Amy Jordan of Amy J Delightful (amyjdelightful.blogspot.com) for her friendship and graphic design expertise.

My readers who encourage me to keep on writing and sharing my heart.

May God be glorified and His Word become flesh in all who read.

About the Author

Kathy L. Gossen seeks to encourage others to live for Jesus in the every day no matter what the occasion. She is frequently found living out this motto as Executive Director of *Central Oklahoma Homeschool Choirs*, blogger/owner of *Cornerstone Confessions,* and host of a weekly home Bible study group. She is the author of *Encompass Preschool Curriculum* and co-author of *iBlog.* Kathy and her husband, Daniel, have two precious little girls and live in Edmond, Oklahoma.

Where you can find Kathy:

- Her blog: *http://cornerstoneconfessions.com*
- G+: +KathyGossen
- Pinterest: @CornerstoneKat
- Facebook: @cornerstoneconfessions
- Twitter: @kathygossen

Made in the USA
Charleston, SC
29 January 2015